White Pearl and I

A Memoir of a Political Refugee

By
Svetlana Kim

ENDORSEMENTS

"This passionate saga of one woman's journey to find freedom illuminates the deepest good in the human soul. Svetlana Kim's unlikely path takes her from Leningrad to Wall Street and beyond, reminding us that pursuing our dreams remains our most powerful path to success."

— Sarah Miller Caldicott, great grandniece of Thomas Edison, co-author of *Innovate Like Edison: The Five-Step System to Breakthrough Business Success*

"Enlightening and entertaining...All at the same time! Svetlana writes with vivid emotion, humor, and hard-hitting and uplifting messages. *White Pearl and I* is a story of love, perseverance, persistence, and happiness as well as meaning and a sense of purpose."

— Grand Master Jhoon Rhee, American Tae Kwon Doe Founding Father, and Martial Arts Instructor for Bruce Lee and Muhammad Ali

"Profound. Provocative. Moving. Prepare to be inspired as you read this page-turning story that showcases what can happen when you face life with initiative, determination and, above all, a commitment to excel and serve others. Read it and reap."

— Sam Horn, author of *Tongue Fu!* and *POP! Create the Perfect Pitch, Title and Tagline for Anything*

"An extraordinary personal account about an unknown history of people displaced by the great political events of the twentieth century. Svetlana Kim's *White Pearl and I* is a true human drama which adds greatly to our understanding of the legacy of forced migration and cultural birth."

— Y. David Chung, film director, and co-producer of *Koryo Saram: The Unreliable People*, winner Best Documentary National Film Board of Canada

"It requires more than soaring prosewriting to produce a wonder such as *White Pearl and I.* Svetlana Kim and her book are one and the same. The passion, willpower, resilience, humor and abiding faith expressed on the pages are the same qualities found in Ms. Kim. Here is a book to remind us all of the powerful call of America across the oceans and to be better people and not take all that we have for granted. I'm a better person because of fellow writer Svetlana Kim."

— Ron Powers, Pulitzer Prize-winning journalist and author of *Mark Twain: A Life*. With James Bradley, he co-wrote the 2000 #1 *New York Times* Bestseller *Flags of Our Fathers*

"Told with honest simplicity and delightfully innocent humor, the plot of *White Pearl and I* reads a bit like a fairy tale. There is a sort of ogre, a few white knights and fairy godmothers, as well as a heroine who, armed with little more than great courage, good luck and a protective aura from her ancestors, triumphs. But this ogre, these knights and magic-makers, and, most of all, this heroine surpass their fictional counterparts because they are real. All of it actually happened, which not only makes the author, Svetlana Kim, worth reading, but also worth knowing.

"And like the wondrous fairy tales we were fed as children, this one, too, has a deeper meaning. It is not only an amazing memoir about a penniless Korean-Russian immigrant making her way in America, it is also a testament to what is great and noble about this country. It shows us at our best—a place and a people willing to embrace and empower someone who works hard to educate herself, find meaning for herself and take advantage of the opportunities offered her. And for me, that's a whole lot better than happily ever after."

— Simon T. Bailey, author of *Release Your Brilliance*

"The book is inspiring and interesting as an historical document as well as an autobiography. We have read many immigrant stories coming from Europe but never one from the Soviet Union and never from a Korean perspective. Kim's strength—and, at the same time, her sentimental attachment to her grandmother's memory—is a reminder of the need of family support and identity. It should be very meaningful to all the Korean refugees as well as for all of us building a new identity in our new country."

— Philanthropist Eva Haller, with Oprah Winfrey, on the Schools Initiative and Free the Children

"As a diplomat for Korea, I have shared many of my countrymen's experiences and the journeys they have taken and their hardships and successes when I served my country in the U.S., Middle East, South America and Asia. Svetlana and her *babushka*'s tale that enfolds in *White Pearl and I* profoundly illustrates the essence of the Korean people's character—persistence, hard work, 'never say never' attitude, willpower, strong family values and living for the next generation—surviving and flourishing in places you least expect. I have often shared with my children and family my amazement when I encounter Koreans in the remotest parts of the world and how they all seemed to have managed in their own way to better their lives and establish a strong foundation for the generations to come. In this ever-growing global world, I am glad that stories such as *White Pearl and I* are being told and shared both with Koreans, both in Korea and abroad, and others in the global community because I believe we as global citizens have more in common than differences as we continue our life's journey."

— Ambassador Chong-Yul Moon

"This is a book in which a reader can live in America and travel to Russia...It reads like a novel. It grabs your attention from the very first sentence."

— Loula Loi Alafoyiannis, founder, Euro-American Women's Council

"This is Svetlana Kim's masterpiece...the book is a masterpiece and so is her extraordinary life! Kim exhibits respect for her past brought forward with contemporary overlays. If you want to know about perseverance and courage culminating in success and happiness, then read this. Kim embraces a richness of culture without forgetting the price of a rich personal history."

— Phebe Phillips, creatrice of exquisite soft toys and author of *Kitty Pink Pink "A World of Change"* (released August 2009)

"Dare to dream—that is what Svetlana Kim teaches us in her book. *White Pearl and I* is full of inspiring stories and cultural history. This book is an important account of Soviet-Korean history, never before told from a first person perspective. Kim has artfully woven this important, but relatively unknown, part of history into her tale of hope and determination for a better life."

— Dr. Eileen R. Borris, author of *Finding Forgiveness*

"A laugh-and-cry true story…Kim's memory of returning to the values of her Russian-Korean *babushka*, White Pearl, is heartbreaking and inspiring. I hope that everyone will read this extraordinary book."

— Quinn Dalton, author of *Bulletproof Girl* and *Stories from the Afterlife*

"A political refugee who escaped communism and came to America with just a dollar in her pocket and not a word of English in her vocabulary, Svetlana Kim will take away your excuse for not making the most of your potential. Follow her basic roadmap; the willingness to give of yourself and focus on providing value to others, and you'll find yourself surrounded by friends who love you and a huge increase in income."

— Bob Burg, co-author of *The Go-Giver* and *Go-Givers Sell More*

947.21
KIM 26
bio
/

To my loving *babushka,* White Pearl

"If I know what love is, it is because of you."
—Hermann Hesse

OUR FAMILY TREE

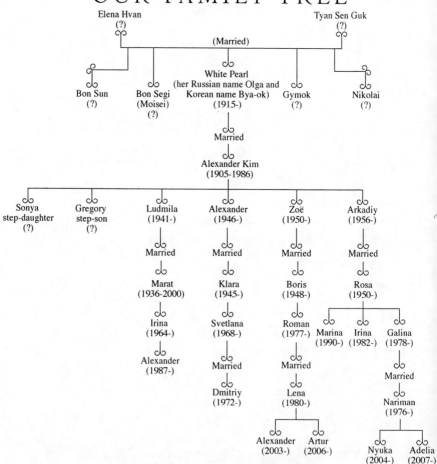

CONTENTS

ACKNOWLEDGMENTS

I once read that every single pearl evolves from a central core. This core is simply an irritant—a fragment of a shell or fishbone, a grain of sand. To protect itself from this irritant, the oyster secretes multiple layers of nacre, which form a beautiful pearl. I think of this process when I think of my grandmother, whose name is White Pearl. She experienced some very difficult events in her life that I will share with you in this book. Despite it all, she became one of the rarest and most beautiful of pearls.

I am grateful to her, my greatest inspiration, my paternal *babushka* ("grandmother" in Russian), White Pearl, who celebrated her ninety-third birthday on January 8, 2008. Also to my late paternal grandfather, Alexander; to my late maternal grandparents, Natasha and Chen Gym; to my parents, Klara and Alexander; to my parents-in-law, Galina and Vladimir; to my wonderful husband, Dmitriy, for his support, enthusiasm, and love; to Dmitriy's maternal grandmother Sofia; and, finally, to my thirty-three nieces and nephews (by the time I finish this book, there may be a few more on the way), who challenged me to write my story.

I am grateful to my friend and mentor Ron Powers, a Pulitzer Prize-winning journalist, novelist, and non-fiction writer and the author of *Mark Twain: A Life*, for encouraging me to bring my story to readers and for being very generous with his time, knowledge, and wisdom.

I am grateful to my friend Sam Horn, for taking time to read the first set of rough and unorganized pages that outlined this book about my life. Sam, thank you for taking a risk and opening many doors for me. I am grateful to Robyn Freedman Spizman for her counseling and support when I was taking my first baby steps writing my book. I am grateful to my editor, Virginia M. Clark, for her keen eye for words. I give endless thanks to Karen Schmitt. Thank you, Karen, for your suggestions that were always critical to my intentions. My heartfelt thanks to an amazing team at BookSurge publishing: Sarah Lange Davis, Sarah Southerland, Lauren Woolley, and Angela Johnson for taking care of the complicated aspects of producing this book.

I deeply appreciate Sonya Sungeui Lee, Reference

Specialist, Korean Section, Asian Division, at the Library of Congress, for her interest in my book, and I am grateful to Dr. James Billington, Librarian of Congress, for opening a section on the Soviet Koreans and for his lifelong interest in Russian history and culture. Because of their support, the Korean Section has a new exhibit entitled, "Soviet Koreans."

A special thanks to Dr. Ross King, Professor, Department of Asian Studies, Korean Language and Literature, at the University of British Columbia for sharing his research. There are roughly 500,000 ethnic Koreans who live in the former USSR today. Like me, they speak the Russian language. Being a Soviet Korean was a "taboo," though, and they were left out of all official surveys of minority issues. The taboo status meant that it was impossible to do any research. As a result, many scholars in Russia had to fight with the Soviet bureaucracy. It was even harder for scholars outside the former USSR to conduct research. In 1987, Dr. Ross King applied through the International Research and Exchanges Board (IREX) to conduct his Harvard doctoral research on the dialect of the Soviet Korean ethnic minority. It took him two years to get permission on the Soviet side.

The Joseon Dynasty (July 1392–August 1910),

which lasted approximately five centuries, ended when the Japan-Korea Annexation Treaty was enforced by the Empire of Japan. Many very poor peasants considered Siberia, a vast land rich in resources, to be the place where they could lead happier lives. As early as 1863, thirteen Korean families moved to the Far East of Russia (FER). In 1900, my paternal great-grandparents moved to Yuzhno-Sakhalinsk, and my grandmother White Pearl was born in 1915 in the city of Suchan (Partizansk today), near Vladivostok. In the fall of 1937, when my grandmother was twenty-two years old, Joseph Stalin ordered a deportation of nearly 200,000 Koreans to Central Asia in the former USSR. My grandmother is one of the survivors of this deportation.

Unfortunately, many community leaders were executed and hundreds of people, including children, perished on the way to Central Asia. Until the era of *glasnost* and *perestroika*, it was prohibited to mention the deportation of Soviet Koreans. Many generations lost the use of the Korean language when Stalin ordered the burning of all Korean textbooks and closed all Korean schools in 1937.

Dr. German Kim has studied the Soviet Koreans and writes more of their story:

... for the Koryo Saram, who have no nation-state, nor local autonomy in either Russia or the newly independent Central Asian states, there is the problem of survival as a unique ethnos. The Koreans of the Far East were the first people of the Soviet Union to be deported, after which the same fate was shared by dozens of other populations. It is wrong to think that Stalin spontaneously decided to deport the Koreans. Top secret order number 1428-326cc of the Soviet government and Communist Party, dated August 21, 1937, [stated that] "the deportation of the Korean population of the Far East signed by Molotov and Stalin was a logical continuation of earlier Czarist and Soviet policy relating to national minority populations." (Dr. German Kim, "Koryo Saram, or Koreans of the Former Soviet Union in the Past and Present," http://www.koryosaram. freenet.kz/).

I would like to thank Steven Lee, who was among

the first-ever group of Fulbright students in 2001–2002 to be sent to the Central Asian republics. His research project, based in Almaty, Kazakhstan, and Tashkent, Uzbekistan, compared Soviet-Korean and Korean-American literature and art, paying particular attention to Soviet national policy (see http://www.sslee.freenet.kz/).

I deeply appreciate my friends: Ingrid Goesnar, Dr. Gloria B. Herndon, Amy E. Hauser, Regina Mead, Lourdes C. Cavalier, Jamie Borromeo, Darlene Mar, Soohyun "Julie" Koo, Kort Borg, Jenny Hou, the entire Westcott-Lahar family, the entire Marsico family, the entire Fraser family, the entire Lasko family, Jim Brennock, Wayne Hower, Françoise and Remi Vespa, Hoang Taing, Phebe Phillips and Mac Hargrove, Jenny Shtipelman, Angella Savage, Jean C. Palmer, Susan I. Wranik, Detta Voesar, late Dr. Andrea O. Sigler, late Donzel Culp, Ann-Marie Triolo, Doug Patterson, Jamey Bradbury, Julianna Baggott, Dr. Hwa-wei Lee, Reme A. Grefalda, Mari Nakahara, Anchi Hoh, Judy S. Lee, Josie Olympia, Lida Peterson, Cynthia and Vinod Shelth, Lani Hay, Judith Willson, Amy DeLeo, Mary MacDonald, Pat Lynch, Christian Oh, Hannah Kim, and Sandy Butler Weil for enriching my life.

Last but not least, I am indebted to the many

American families who opened their homes to me, treated me to McDonald's, and bought me bus passes. Let me thank those before me and those still to come.

Now I want to take you to Russia with me. To start this journey, turn the page.

Svetlana Kim

Washington, D.C.

May 25, 2008

CHAPTER 1
AN INNOCENT TRIP TO A
LOCAL BAKERY

"The Chinese use two brush strokes
to write the word 'crisis.' One brush
stroke stands for 'danger'; the other for
'opportunity.' In a crisis, be aware of the
danger—but recognize the opportunity."

—John F. Kennedy

It all started with a loaf of bread that didn't even exist. It was early afternoon in Leningrad, a freezing winter day in December 1991 that felt more like night. Everything was dark gray—the sky, the buildings, the people's moods. *Another gloomy day*, I thought, pulling my scarf to cover my chin and nose from the cold wind, which was blowing into my face so hard that I could not keep my eyes open. I was standing in line at the bakery for the third day in a row. The previous two days, after I had waited for hours, the owner had reluctantly ducked outside the door to announce, "There won't be a bread delivery. You might as well go home." The bakery was the size of the kitchen in my apartment, with one counter for the cash register and bare shelves that should have been filled with baked goods. By the register, below the sign for *sahar* (sugar), sat a few lonely brown bags empty of sugar. The scarcity of bread, potatoes, and vodka was maddening. Milk, cheese, meat, and sugar became difficult to find in stores. Soaps and toothpastes, shampoos and razor blades vanished from store shelves.

To be a resident of Leningrad, you had to have a *propiska* (a record of place of residence). The *propiska* system was similar to the czarist internal passport system used to control population movements in the Russian Empire. If I wanted to move to Moscow, I needed a *propiska* in Moscow to be a legal resident there. Yet becoming a legal resident is still not easy, even in Russia in today's free market, when people cannot only buy apartments but can also build homes and castles.

I read that the Bolsheviks abolished the passport system right after the October Revolution, but Joseph Stalin reinstated it in December 1932. When I still lived in Russia, you needed a valid *propiska* stamp in your passport in order to get a job, get married, or receive medical treatments, which were free for all citizens. This may be different now, but back then, if you didn't have your *propiska*, you didn't receive ration coupons, either. Each month, my ration coupons allowed me to buy two bars of soap, a pound of butter, a pound of any kind of meat, and one box of detergent. I didn't dare to lose them. I hand washed all of my clothes because we didn't have a washing machine. I washed my clothes, towels, and bedding and hung them to dry on the balcony.

Every Saturday I went to the *banya*, the traditional steam bath. I didn't like the heat of the *parilka* (steam room) my very first time, but eventually I got used to it and even learned how to take a cold shower afterward. However, I enjoyed the health benefits of hitting my body with the *venik*, a bunch of dried and leafy twigs from birch trees. In fact, this process was known for increasing blood circulation. My *venik* smelled like fresh-cut grass in my grandparents' garden on a bright sunny morning. I felt thirsty, exhausted, and very hot right after I left the *parilka*. According to Russian tradition, the men would drink beer after their visit to the *parilka;* the women would have a glass of *kvass* (a nonalcoholic beverage made from dark rye bread), which is still a very popular drink in Eastern Europe. After an hour of rest, my body cooled down, and I was rejuvenated. I felt peaceful and serene. I was not surprised to read recently that visiting the *banya* in Moscow and riding the *troika* (a three-horse sled) were very popular with foreign tourists visiting Russia.

By the third day at the bakery in Leningrad, the mood in line was different. Instead of everyone complaining about the lack of bread, the older people and the students (the only people with time to wait in the long lines) were talking anxiously about the political changes announced the previous evening on *Novosti,* a TV news program.

"The Wall is coming down," said one woman with astonishment. Her fur coat had buttons of different sizes, and the sleeves were too short. I could tell that her life was not easy. I noticed her beautiful eyes. They were the color of a winter sky, neither gray nor blue. An empty mesh bag hung on her left arm, and she was trying to keep her hands in her pockets. "I will prepare my cash now," she said and looked at me. "It is worth more now than after the war."

"Gorbachev is resigning," said a man who looked like a typical professor, wearing round glasses with thick lenses and clutching a book under his arm. "Why did we have a revolution in 1917? We don't even have bread now. This is going to be a long day." He turned to me. "Do you know that we are not the RSFRS [Russian Soviet Federated Socialist Republic] any longer? The whole country will collapse. What a shame! It has existed for seventy-four years. Your generation will never comprehend what we lived through."

"It will get better," I said, without the slightest note of interest. I looked at his many-times-washed plastic bag, which held another newspaper and *Novyi Mir* (*New World*, a popular literary magazine). *He loves to read*, I noticed. *He may be right that it will be a long day.*

"The economy is going to collapse," another man behind me added gloomily. He lit another cigarette every fifteen minutes, complaining about his lack of appetite. He said, "I don't mind standing in line to get a loaf of bread, but I'll die if they discontinue selling Belomorkanal [an inexpensive brand of cigarettes]." I remembered the summer of last year when an acute shortage of cigarettes provoked riots in many cities in Russia.

All I wanted was a loaf of bread. *What does this mean?* I wondered. The government had always proclaimed Russia to be the best country in the world. Most of us innocently, patriotically, completely, and unquestioningly believed it. If our economy was collapsing, if Russia could no longer even provide bread for its citizens, what would happen to us? How would these changes affect us? Little did I know how much my own life was about to change.

The small group at the bakery suddenly stopped talking. Everyone turned around and began to stare with a mixture of awe and fear at something behind me. I looked around to see what had caused them to fall silent. A sleek black Mercedes 500 had pulled up to the curb. The driver rolled down the tinted window and yelled at the group, "*Narod* [people]! Do we have *hleb* [bread] or do we have to eat *kartoshku* [potatoes]?"

I laughed aloud. Who did I see at the wheel of this fancy car but my old classmate Vladimir? He hadn't changed much. Even though it was a gray winter day, he was wearing oversized, too-cool-for-school Versace sunglasses and a long leather coat. His blue jeans and his new pair of Adidas were my dream. I looked at what I was wearing: a black rabbit fur coat and a sable hat, made by my mother. I looked at Vladimir again. *Russian Mafia.* It didn't surprise me. Even back in high school, we all knew Vladimir was not destined for a life as a doctor, professor, or scientist. Bored and aimless, he was our resident "bad boy." He had dropped out and joined the army, but after that no one knew what had happened to him. His luxury automobile, a rarity in our area, answered any questions anyone might have had about his current line of work.

Vladimir beckoned to me and asked what I was doing.

"I'm a student at Leningrad State University," I told him.

"What about the others?" he asked. "What is Ludmila doing?"

He pulled out a new pack of Marlboros, tapped it on his left palm, took out a cigarette, and lit it with a silver lighter. *My father used matches that cost him one kopeika per box. We used to buy fifty matches at once,* I thought, looking at Vladimir.

I remembered that Vladimir had had a crush on Ludmila.

"He's not my type," Ludmila had always said. Her parents would do anything for her if she were married to the "right" man. According to her father, Vladimir was not right for her. She was an only child. Her family spent every summer in London, and she always came back wearing fashionable black jeans and a Burberry coat, hat, scarf, gloves, and carrying a gorgeous leather handbag. I don't think many of her friends understood her European fashions.

"They just don't get it," Ludmila said. "Burberry is the most respected brand in Europe right now." I remembered the days when she used to shop at Detskiy Mir, a children's store. Nowadays Ludmila was still under ninety pounds and looked like Kate Moss. *If she were to see Vladimir now, would she like him?* I wondered.

"Did she get married?" he asked.

"No. She immigrated to the United States. She actually sent me a letter last year and invited me to come live with her in New York. It was the strangest thing," I told him truthfully, still amazed that she had been able to track me down. "A young man I didn't even know just walked up to me at the university one day and said, 'I've got a letter for you.'"

Vladimir puffed on his cigarette.

"I told him, 'A letter for me? From whom?' He shrugged, handed it to me, and left without saying another word."

"Ludmila asked you to come live with her?" Vladimir sounded shocked. "Are you going to take her up on her offer?"

"You must be joking. You know I don't speak English. How would I earn a living there? Plus, it's almost impossible to get an airline ticket."

To my amazement, he said, "I've got a ticket for a plane that's leaving for New York on December 18. You can have it for forty-five thousand rubles. One of my regular clients, a businessman who makes tons of money and goes to New York like I go to Moscow, canceled his trip."

"Forty-five thousand rubles!" I gasped. "Why so expensive?" December 18 was less than a week away. Could I get a visa in time?

"Don't you know?" Vladimir looked at me as if I were a dunce. "Aeroflot only issues round-trip tickets for international flights or travelers with guest visas."

Regardless of the price, I knew that a future I'd only dreamed of had just materialized. My impulse to say, "I'll take the ticket!" was immediately followed by a flurry of concerns. Where would I find the money? How could I possibly abandon my family, my friends, and everything I knew? Suddenly, I went from being daunted by the seemingly impossible task to being determined to pull it off. "I want the ticket," I told Vladimir, projecting a bravado I didn't fully feel.

He scoffed. "You can't afford it. I am one of the top dealers in the black market. Didn't you hear on the news that Aeroflot sells its airline tickets for U.S. dollars only? It will cost you even more because you have to convert your rubles into dollars."

"Are you Mafia?" I asked him outright, thinking that was the only way he could have gotten access to this ticket.

"Not really. I like money. And I make good money. And I help people make good money."

"I will buy your ticket. It's a done deal," I told him emphatically, not even knowing where I would find the money, just knowing that I would.

"The deal is not done until I have the cash in my hands."

I assured him that I would have the money. We agreed to meet at eight o'clock the night of the flight.

I raced off on my mission to somehow collect the cash, pack my belongings, and go to the consulate to beg, plead, and pray for a visa, which was the linchpin on which my new future hinged. First, I called my parents. My mother answered the phone. She was working a night shift at the hospital.

"Mom," I shouted, because telephone reception was usually bad, "I'm going to New York!"

"What?" she asked, caught off guard.

"Mama, I'm serious. I cannot call you from New York. It's too expensive." Words tumbled out of my mouth as I tried to explain about connecting with Vladimir, and that I was going to America to stay with Ludmila and that I needed money, lots of money—their entire savings, in fact, to buy the plane ticket.

It was too much, too fast for my mother. "Go to bed. Are you drunk?" She laughed and hung up the phone.

Next, I started visiting friends to ask for money. Some of them did not have a ruble to their name; others gave me what they could. Either way, I understood. As a student, my monthly *stipendia* (scholarship) was a measly two dollars, and here I was asking for hundreds of dollars more. I took a train to see Lena who was very well off and a best friend of my cousin Irina. My cousin and I walked into Lena's communal apartment with one big kitchen that looked very commercial and had very old ovens, probably from Stalin's era.

"Where are you going to stay in New York?" Lena asked.

"I have a friend who moved there a few years ago."

"I was in Germany this summer," Lena said. "I didn't know if I could ever learn how to speak German, but I did. Do you speak English?"

"I've studied German for at least twelve years," I replied, "but I don't speak English at all." I felt like I was being interviewed for a job.

"Well, if you learned German, you can learn English. The hardest thing is to get a visa. I will give you all I can." Lena went to her room and came back with some cash. "Here. *Udachi* [good luck]!"

"*Bolshoe spasibo* [thank you very much]! I didn't even expect that much." I had never held so much money in my hands. I was grateful to Lena for showing such venture-capitalist spirit to lend me money for half of my airline ticket. (And eventually she was paid back.)

I was almost to my goal of forty-five thousand rubles!

In the midst of all this scurrying to collect the money, I carved out some time to go to the U.S. Consulate. A long line snaked out the front door. After I had stood in line for hours, they closed for the day. The next morning, I took no chance and was one of the first ones to queue up. Everyone was talking excitedly about reuniting with family members overseas. My heart sank when I realized that they all had grandparents, aunts, or uncles living in America, which meant they were more likely to get a visa than I was. The longer I waited, and the more I heard, the smaller I felt. Everyone was telling elaborate stories about the months it had taken for their relatives to get their visas and how expensive it was to live in New York City. What nerve I had to believe I could pull this off. Who was I, after all? A simple student. I wasn't wealthy. I wasn't famous. I wasn't a model. I didn't have anyone waiting for me in America—no one waiting to sponsor or support me once I arrived. What was I thinking? As the day wore on, my anxiety increased. I noticed that a number of individuals who had arrived hours after I had were being called ahead of me.

Puzzled, I turned to the man next to me. He just rubbed his fingers together in the age-old symbol for bribe. How naïve I was. I knew what I had to do. That evening at home, after another futile day at the consulate, I took out the gold earrings and necklace my grandmother had given me months before.

To White Pearl, and no one else, I had confessed my crazy dream of going to the United States. We talked about the out-of-the-blue invitation to go to America I had received from Ludmila. I recounted another story when I went to Moscow for a day with my father in 1990. We ate at McDonald's in Pushkin Square, waiting more than an hour to get in. And once we did, all the seats were taken, so we went to the park to eat our burgers. In Russia, it is considered bad manners to eat or drink in public. Waiting at McDonald's, I had wondered, *Why do they call it fast food?* McDonald's served food that looked like my grandmother's *kotlety* (minced pork with onions on a bun).

"I want to go to McDonald's in New York City," I told White Pearl. "I want to see Liza Minnelli sing on Broadway. I want to stroll through Central Park, to continue my education in America, and someday start my own business. I want a better life."

Instead of telling me I was being foolish, instead of dismissing my wishes as being unrealistic, my grandmother encouraged me to accept Ludmila's invitation. She knew what it meant to want a better life—and also what it was like to have a dream taken away.

CHAPTER 2
MY RUSSIAN-KOREAN BABUSHKA

"People don't alter history any
more than birds alter the sky;
they just make brief patterns in it."
—Terry Pratchett

❦

My paternal grandmother, Bya-ok ("White Pearl"), was born on January 8, 1915, and christened with the Russian name, Olga. As a young woman, her hair was jet black, her eyes radiated pure love, her skin was the color of a lustrous white pearl, her lips were full, her smile was irresistible, her voice was soft and pleasant, and her touch was gentle. Her laugh was inspiring and contagious. Her children called her "Mama" and her husband, my grandfather Alexander, called her simply "Olya." To me, she was always my loving *babushka*.

In the cold autumn of 1900, after a poor harvest and famine in Korea, White Pearl's parents, Elena Hvan and Tyan Sen Guk, had come to Russia to pursue a better life. They arrived at Sakhalin Island in the far eastern part of Russia. White Pearl told me, "My parents were country people, affable and down-to-earth, and of course hard working. They were poor like everyone else, but poverty back then was not depressing as it is today. My parents had neither electricity nor plumbing, neither bath nor shower. In order to stay clean, they melted snow in the winter to wash themselves. In the summer, they swam in rivers or lakes. They used kerosene lamps and were considered rich by their neighbors."

My great-grandparents were the first generation of what we call Koryo-Saram, which means "Korean person," the people who came to Russia during the Joseon (also Choson or Chosun) Dynasty. Chosun is an ancient name for Korea that means "Land of the Morning Calm." As early as 1861, thirteen Korean families applied for permission to settle in Russia. Most of them were very poor peasants who faced death, hunger, and freezing winters. The weather was severe, not unlike it is today. They kept their Korean lifestyle, cooked Korean food, spoke the Korean language, and wore traditional Korean clothes.

"My father built a *kamya*," White Pearl told me. "It was a rock oven with a big iron pot placed right on the top. Later he installed a cast-iron cook stove. My mother cooked outside the house when weather was mild in the summer and early fall. We enjoyed having supper in the small backyard. Elena made tasty food. My mother cooked two meals a day, breakfast and supper. She worked quickly and never wasted anything. Elena cooked rice, *tyai tyamur* [miso soup], *kimchi*, long noodles, and rice cakes from sticky rice. She fed the bones and leftovers—if any—to the dogs. She crushed eggshells and used them to fertilize the plants. The water used to wash rice was also used for plants, potato skins were cooked and fed to the chickens, and dried bread was fed to the horses. My brothers and I loved to bake potatoes and freshly gathered pinecones in the ashes. Our mother germinated beans in a medium-sized bowl placed in a dark corner in our house for a week, generously watering them two times a day, early in the morning and late at night. Fresh crunchy sprouts were the only fresh produce we ate during the winter," White Pearl said, trying to recall her mother's recipes. "Bean sprouts provided high-quality protein. My mother stir-fried them, added them to soups, and mixed them with fresh ginger root."

White Pearl's mother polished her iron pots with sand. She had no glass dishes, only enamel plates and big cups, a wooden ladle, a *kuksipuntur* (a machine to make long noodles), and some cups made from pumpkin shells for measuring grains and flour.

"My mother," said White Pearl, showing me the only existing photograph of her mother, "wore the same clothes every day. A white smock, a long skirt, white cotton socks, and straw shoes. Her clothes looked as clean and neat as she did herself. As I was growing up, my clothes resembled my mother's—clean, neat, well ironed, and spotless. My mother always remained loving and optimistic about her life."

Elena made clothes for her husband, her kids, and herself by hand. She knitted hats and gloves and repaired holes on the elbows of sweaters that were passed down from the oldest daughter, Gymok, to the youngest son, Nikolai.

"Three years after my parents' arrival in Russia," Grandmother said after a pause, "they built a thriving community. Their life seemed to be normal again. They were happy with their new life in a new country.

Koreans called Russia their motherland.

"I only had one photo of my cherished mother, Elena," White Pearl continued. "I want you to have it. I regret that I don't have any pictures of my father. He was a good man. I inherited many qualities from him: a strong work ethic, ambition, and humility. My mother played a big role in my life. She was the one who taught me to be a good wife and mother. I was born in a small town of Suchan in the *Dalnevostochnyi Krai* [a maritime region]. In my day, we had Pacific monsoons, constant gusts of wind, and temperatures dropping below thirty-seven degrees centigrade. Our region was the main outlet to the Pacific Ocean. It was close to the city of Vladivostok.

"I was married once to a man I did not love," my grandmother confessed. "I divorced him in 1937, the year I was deported from Vladivostok to the city of Kzyl-Orda, Kazakhstan. Our good friend introduced me to my second husband in the winter of 1937. I married your grandfather, a widower at thirty years old who was devastated by the loss of his wife. His only daughter, Sonya, died at the age of nineteen from meningitis. She was just a newlywed.

"When Sonya died," she said, and her voice sounded startled, "I heard our dogs barking and barking all night long. It's not a good sign, since dogs bark when someone dies. I was home alone, and early the next morning, I received a *telegramma* [telegram] about Sonya's death.

"Your parents are second-generation Koreans who were born and raised in the Soviet Union [USSR]. Your father was born the year after the end of World War II. He was my second child. Sasha [Alexander] was healthy and caused me no troubles. Sasha had excellent grades in mathematics and physics, like your Auntie Luda. I knew he would be a doctor or an engineer.

"When your father was old enough to work, he helped his papa in the fields loading rice sacks onto the trucks. The sacks were heavy. Even the horses were tired after a long day. Growing rice is a very labor-intensive process that also required plenty of water and rainfall. When we first arrived in Kzyl-Orda in the fall of 1937, only *kamysh* [reed grass] was growing, there were no trees or bushes. But three years later, our fields flourished with rice. We also used the rice fields for breeding catfish. Once the rice fields were drained, the plots were especially fertile since the soil was free of dangerous worms and bugs. Many farmers preferred to lease their rice fields to grow vegetables. All our tools—plows, forks, and shovels—were handmade. You couldn't buy seeds. Your grandfather saved ripe tomatoes, crushed them in the *seto* [sieve], and separated the seeds from the skin and pulp. He washed them in a mesh bag until they were clean and then dried them in the shade on an old table that we had had for as long as I could remember. The dried seeds were stored in cotton drawstring bags and hidden away in a dry, dark, and secure place, safe from starving rodents, until March of the following year."

❧

White Pearl told me about Stalin's mandate to burn all books, including textbooks, that were printed in Korean. "The people tried to save their language and their culture. The villagers copied stories and lessons by hand into twelve-page notebooks, and they wrote down the words to Korean songs so they could teach their children. I gave my copies to your Aunt Luda. You used to understand Koryo-mar when you were little." Grandmother looked proud. "I taught you how to speak Koryo-mar, but your father wanted you to speak Russian first.

"My mother, Elena, and my father, Tyan Sen Guk, didn't speak Russian when they arrived on Sakhalin Island from Korea. But they wanted a better life, just like you. They learned how to speak Russian, and you will learn how to speak English," White Pearl said.

"My father built a log house by hand from pine logs for the summer and a *zemlyanka* [underground dwelling] for winter. It kept us warm. The summer house usually had one or two rooms. A low, wooden Korean-style table, covered with *kleenka* [oilcloth] secured to the top with tiny nails, stood in the middle of our room. A small stove was in the far left corner, a *moktusai* [handmade stool] for adults, and round pillows for children were nearby. Wet mittens, scarves, hats, boots, and coats were dried on the stool near the oven."

Their dinners were very simple: *seryagi*, a broth with cabbage, a little bit of rice, *kimchi*, and fried fish. Everyone sat on the floor cross-legged or on their knees, and after dinner, the table was wiped off and set against the wall to convert the kitchen into a bedroom. The kids slept together in one room, sharing two mattresses and two warm blankets and two pillows stuffed with herbs or seeds. Winter was a time for socializing and being lazy. Like her mother, White Pearl was a good seamstress. She kept her bobbins, needles, threads, scissors, and buttons in an empty gooseberry jam jar. Women knitted and sewed and baked and cleaned. Men went hunting when the weather permitted. The village was small, maybe twenty families, no more.

"We kept a few dogs, for winter transport,"

Grandmother said. "Once, when a *buran* [blizzard] was howling all night long, we let the dogs in. It was too cold even for them outside. In the morning, we woke up in complete darkness. We couldn't open the door. We were trapped under a *sugrob* [mountain of snow] about a meter high. Our neighbors had to shovel it off to open our front door."

Her parents grew millet and cabbage that looked different from the cabbage we have today. They pressed their own oil from sesame seeds and stored homemade goose fat for long winters. Poorer families grew potatoes to replace rice, which kept them alive when food was scarce. Her mother, Elena, cooked small potatoes in a big pot to feed pigs, cows, and ducks. Many peasants were skeptical when it came to potatoes. They called them "devil's apples" because so many people had been poisoned by eating the leaves instead of the roots. They just didn't know how to prepare the potatoes. They also dried and smoked salmon and other small fish. Elena gave her kids fish oil because it was good for their health, although they hated the taste of it.

"There was no one who didn't like my mother's rice porridge," Grandmother remembered fondly. "We ate it for breakfast, and according to custom, it was given as nourishment to the sick.

"I had one older sister, Gymok, and three brothers, Bon Sun, Bon Segi (Moisey was his Russian name), and Bon Hak (Nikolai was his Russian name). One morning, before the sun came up, a group of us went down to the ocean shore to gather seaweed. A black and tan German shepherd attacked us. Someone shrieked, 'Dog!' But it was too late. The dog jumped on the back of a tiny woman and bit her on her neck."

"That is absolutely horrible, Grandma." I shook my head in disbelief. "It's so cruel."

"Well, the people who lived there didn't want us to pick up the seaweed. But nothing would stop us because we were determined to feed our kids and raise our families. Seaweed was very important for their health. I learned how to pick edible mushrooms, *oblipiha* [sea buckthorn or Siberian pineapple—small, bright orange-colored berries], cranberries, gooseberries, and flowers. I loved the blue-purple flowers you can see through the snow. They were the first to bloom...in a hurry to see the sun," she said with great love. "Flowers bloomed like crazy. You would be afraid to walk because flower buds were everywhere. I loved to sit on a rock and admire the flowers, or listen to the murmur of a nearby creek, or the birds' songs. I watched the gentle breezes stir the grass, hares chase each other, and deer watch over their brood. Sometimes I caught a glimpse of whales. Springtime was fresh and alive with wildlife. In May, deer usually gave birth to one or maybe three fawns. In March, the hares behaved like kids, boxing each other during mating rituals. When autumn arrived, I enjoyed the *listopad* [falling leaves]. The entire countryside looked like a kaleidoscope. During the winter months, I enjoyed watching the snowfall and the hares zigzagging through the vast fields. The local tribesmen fished and hunted, but only for sea animals, especially seals. They avoided farming because they believed that would hurt the land.

"From time to time my father made delicious caviar from pike fish. He would ask one of us to hold a glass jar while he would gently press the eggs from the fish's belly. The orange-colored grains of caviar would stream into the jar until it was full.

"My mother added salt on top and placed the jar in a cool place, and in a few days the caviar was ready to eat. My father built a boat and sailed to China in the 1920s, to bring back salt, spices, silk, and clothes. Salt-making was an ancient industry in China and many Chinese people worked at the salt mines. I remember that salt was very expensive, but it was essential to our survival. We needed it to pickle vegetables, like cabbage, as well as fish and meat. My father would sell the goods he imported to the villagers and then go back to China to buy more."

White Pearl's older sister, Gymok, married a good man from Seoul whose father was a pharmacist. Her husband went to medical school and studied abroad. "I remember when she was ready to get married," Grandmother marveled. "Our mother, who was an excellent cook, told her, 'The path to a man's heart lies through his stomach.'

"I think that Gymok was the most beautiful of all of us. She had long straight legs, which was quite unusual for Asian women. When she got married, I cried all day because I didn't want her to leave our house. We were very close. It also meant that I was next in line even though I was still young. My sister was very lucky to marry a good man," she said and went back to her story.

"Young people didn't choose their future spouses," White Pearl said. "The girl's father acted as the negotiator. If a family had no *pridannoe* [dowry] to offer, his daughter became a servant. If the father had at least a quarter of his wealth in assets, like horses, gold coins, and land, and money for the dowry, his daughter could marry well."

Even today, my grandmother tells me how much she loved Gymok. I never met her before she died. Sometimes, I try to imagine what she was like. She must have been a special person because my ninety-three-year-old grandmother still talks about her. I regret we have no photos of Gymok. It was a long time ago, and I don't think they had cameras back then.

Eventually, Gymok's husband became a president of the village council. My grandmother thinks that he went back to Korea after the turmoil of 1937, the year of deportation. She heard that her sister was sent to Tashkent, Uzbekistan, at that time. Gymok died in the late 1960s.

"My father was called a *kulak* [rich peasant], as he was becoming financially well off. Prior to the October Revolution of 1917, he owned his livestock and his home, and even employed others. He paid his workers well. Villagers typically worked for meager salaries or none at all; most worked in exchange for food or wood.

"In 1926, my father and my older brother, Bon Sun, went to China to sell local products in the Chinese markets. Upon their return, the profits were to be distributed to the villagers who had entrusted them with goods. But they encountered a terrible storm and the boat was wrecked. Their bags—filled with seaweed, dried salmon, Siberian ginseng roots [raw ginseng was chewed to fight disease] and sable skins—were washed away into the ocean. My father and my older brother were gone for three long years," Grandmother said. "My mother was left all by herself with four children. Strangers would come to our house and ask our mother to pay them back. They would sit quietly and not say a word for a few hours and then leave. But we had no money. My mother could not even afford to make an extra portion of rice porridge for our neighbors. No one visited us. But three years later, my father and brother came back from China, they paid off their debt, and they brought many goodies. And they had a bigger boat," White Pearl continued.

"The Bolsheviks rejected the ideas of individual farming and prosperity for the peasants. They believed in socialist agriculture. Stalin initiated collective farming throughout the Soviet Union in 1929 when he ordered the annihilation of the *kulaks*. He confiscated their land and property, and caused the tragic death of millions of ordinary, hard-working people. My father and his older son, Bon Segi, left for China. It was in February of 1931."

"How did they cross the border?" I could not understand how they could escape to China.

"He got a sleigh and a horse—a gorgeous, well-groomed chestnut. The whole countryside, including the Amur River, was blanketed in snow. My father whipped the horse and it took off like the wind. The sleigh became a tiny ball as it slowly disappeared in the distance on the other side of the Amur. I still remember that day like it was yesterday. The Communists closed the border, and I never saw them again."

"What did your father say to you before he left?" I was trying to imagine the scene when my grandmother saw her father and brother for the last time in her life.

"He gave me a hug and asked me to take care of my little brother, Nikolai."

White Pearl went to her jewelry box and carefully drew out the earrings and necklace that my grandfather had given her many years ago. The earrings were oval-shaped, solid gold with Byzantine-style filigree. The necklace was a simple chain. She gently placed them in my hands.

"Take these," she said, wrapping my fingers around them. "If going to America is your dream, maybe these can help. If you ever suffer hardship, sell them. Remember, doing nothing is also a risk. The world is open to you. This is an opportunity of a lifetime."

My grandmother's gifts were always precious. She had made my pillow, my royal blue silk mattress, and my warm winter blanket of silk with a pink dahlia print. White Pearl used to buy me sandals, boots, leggings, notes, and pencils for school every year.

Although I was tremendously moved by her magnanimous gesture at that time, I couldn't bring myself to sell her jewelry. Now, holding it and remembering that visit when she had told me so much of our family history, I was immobilized at the prospect of leaving behind everyone and everything I had known all my life, including White Pearl herself.

Memories of my grandmother's generosity flashed through my mind as I gazed at her earrings and necklace. *It's time to take advantage of her gift as she intended,* I said to myself. *If this is what it's going to take to get my name called at the consulate, if this can buy my future, so be it.* I wrapped her treasures in a white handkerchief with small violet flowers embroidered in the right bottom corner. The handkerchief had been made in China and was another gift from my grandmother (her neighbor's granddaughter had gone to China and brought it back for White Pearl). I placed the packet on my dresser. I would wear the jewelry the next day. Rather than passively waiting for fate to take its course, I would do what I could to help it along.

The next morning, I dressed carefully. I put on dark navy trousers, a white shirt, and a bright pink sweater that I had knitted for myself that fall. I didn't want to appear too rich, but I didn't want to appear too poor, either. Then I put on my grandmother's golden earrings and fastened her necklace around my neck. I looked in the mirror, wondering if this would be the first and last time I would wear them, wondering if they would somehow play a role in fulfilling my dream to start a new life in America.

Two blocks away from the consulate, the unthinkable happened. Four young hoodlums with hate-filled faces surrounded me, grabbed my arms, and screamed at me, "You're Japanese. Leave our country." They tore off my earrings, took White Pearl's necklace, pushed me to the ground, and ran off, yelling over their shoulders, "Go back where you came from."

This was the safest area of the city—the Consulate General of the United States of America. I had been here the previous night. I saw men in business suits walking around the consulate. I approached a police officer who was standing at the end of the block, but he didn't care to file a report. People were passing by and no one stopped. In tears, I collapsed onto the curb. I felt sick to my stomach. White Pearl's earrings and necklace were gone. I was in despair. Was this bad luck? An omen? Did this mean I wasn't supposed to go? I sat there in turmoil. Fear grabbed my body. I was numb. I couldn't bear to tell my grandmother that her earrings and necklace had been stolen. But the thought of returning home a failure, my hopes dashed, my dream stolen—well, that wasn't an option either.

It seemed as if my ancestors' determination and resourcefulness, their perseverance in the face of adversity, and their entrepreneurial spirit crystallized in me in that moment. I went from feeling confused to one-hundred-percent clarity. I was going forward. Nothing would be gained by retreating. I would not allow circumstances to defeat me.

My father told me once, "When you get knocked down, you must get up." I bit my lower lip, got up, and walked to the consulate, and wonder of wonders, after an hour of waiting, my name was called.

Before walking into the consulate, I had asked a young man, a ballet dancer I'd been talking with, "How do you say hello in English?"

He said the one magic syllable that was about to play a hand in my fate. "Hi."

"I can say that. How simple. Hi!" I repeated back to him.

"I love New York," he said. "And I was even there last year. I've performed with the Kirov Ballet on several occasions. But I didn't get my visa this time."

"*Gospodi* [Oh, my God]! It is my turn. They called my name." I squared my shoulders and strode into the office. "Hi!" I said brightly.

The man stopped in his tracks, eyes wide open with surprise. "Finally, someone who speaks English. Take a seat," he said warmly, pointing to the chair with a gold leaf frame and silk fabric. It was too pretty to sit in. His shirt was pressed and starched, but he wasn't wearing a jacket or a tie. I could tell he was a good listener. He looked straight into my eyes.

This was going to be a difficult task, to convince him to give me a visa.

I sat on the edge of the chair as I had been taught by my mother. I don't remember the other details of his office because I was so focused on his questions. I looked directly into his eyes to mirror his gestures, though I didn't feel comfortable doing that because it is something we are not accustomed to in my culture. My entire English vocabulary consisted of that one word, learned seconds before. Nonetheless, it seemed to get our meeting off to a positive start, for which I would be eternally grateful.

After a long pause, he switched back to Russian and asked, "What is the reason you want to go to America?"

I told him the truth. "I want to become a successful businesswoman and continue my education in America."

"Do you own a business?"

"No. I'm a student at Leningrad State University."

"Who are your parents?"

"My father is a pulmonologist, and my mother is a midwife."

"Do you have any siblings?"

"No, I am the only child. But I have a cousin who is four years older. I call her my sister. We grew up together and are very close to each other. Her mother is my father's older sister."

"The only child wants to go to America. Do your parents agree?"

"I think so."

He probably thinks that I am not a good child, like his, I thought, judging by his reaction. "Yes, indeed," I said aloud. "I called them last night and asked for lots of money to purchase my airline ticket. Well," I said, puffing up, "going back to your question about a business. I am a partner of a small cooperative that offers classes in German, Finnish, and English. Here is the advertisement I created. It is a great opportunity to earn money because many people are leaving for Israel and America." I handed him my one-page handwritten advertisement with the phone number tabs across the bottom. On one side was a gorgeous drawing of a statue drawn by one of my friends.

"This is a wonderful drawing. Serious artist. Is it your drawing?"

"No, my friend drew it. My partner is the daughter of one of the Secretaries of State," I said, finishing my pitch.

He asked a few more questions about why I wanted to travel to the United States and I answered them honestly and simply. He looked at me speculatively and then seemed to make up his mind.

"You can go to America," he said, signing my documents with a flourish. "Good luck. Your visa will be ready in a few days."

I kissed my red passport before I gave it to a young man standing behind a big desk in the back of the room. I knew that this was just the beginning of my journey. Was I scared? Did I know what awaited me? I could not even imagine in my wildest dreams.

"They're letting me go to America!" I screamed as I ran outside. Everyone was surprised that I got my visa.

"Wait! What did you tell them?" one young woman begged me. "Can you write down the questions they asked you?"

"What is your profession?" an older man asked me. "Do they need physicians in New York City? Did they say anything?"

"What a strange day," a teacher said. "They turned down almost all the applicants. But I still have hope."

"I have to go," I said to everyone, smiling for the first time in the last three days. "Good luck. I hope to see you in New York City one day!"

A youngster pulled at my sleeve. "Do you speak English well?" he asked.

"I know one magic word: Hi."

"That's it? You cannot even say your name in one word. You must be lucky."

"I know," I told him. "Just be confident. Be yourself. You'll be fine."

I put my invitation in a pocket that was deep enough to hold keys, a few bills, and a bit of change. My mother sewed all my clothes with deep pockets. "Thieves can cut a purse and steal your wallet, but no one can steal money from your pockets," she said. I rarely carried paper money in my pocket, mostly just change for the subway or the bus.

I wished I could visit White Pearl again, or at least call her to tell her that she had sent me good luck, but she didn't have a phone. I would send her a letter from America. I had my visa. Now I just needed to collect the rest of the money before meeting Vladimir again.

Gathering a few hundred rubles here, a few hundred rubles there, I finally raised all the cash. My friends all told me that the fee Vladimir was charging was exorbitant, yet we all knew it might be my one and only chance to get out of the country. I made one last quick trip to my apartment and hurriedly packed my belongings, such as they were—a pair of jeans, two pairs of undergarments, two T-shirts, a few books, and a world map. My friend Nina and my cousin Irina had both told me to bring a map of the world. That was a tutorial for my first international voyage to America. A friend of my aunt referred Nina to us. She had spent a few days in Leningrad visiting us from Almaty.

I also had the invitation from my friend Ludmila, and a letter for Galina, Nina's cousin, who was an attorney in Sacramento, California. "This is your destination," Nina had told me, pointing at the map. "San Francisco. You have to go across America. And please give this letter to Galina when you see her," Nina said. "Maybe you can stay with her mother, who lives alone and doesn't speak much English. Galina was a little girl when her family moved to America."

That was it. I glanced at the phone, wanting to call my friends to say good-bye, but there was no time. I had a plane to catch.

I arrived at our meeting place five minutes early, out of breath and filled with anxiety that the whole thing had been a ruse and Vladimir wouldn't show. *He is not here! I can't believe it.*

He finally showed up late. I didn't know what to expect next. I handed over my wad of hard-borrowed cash.

He riffled through it and frowned. "You're one thousand rubles short."

"No!" I gasped. "That's exactly what you told me to bring." I almost broke into tears. After all I had been through, I felt hopeless.

"Well, the price has gone up."

He was blackmailing me. But what choice did I have? I was so close. I couldn't bear to think about it all vanishing. I had given him all my cash and he had my ticket. At that point, it would be easier to raise another one thousand rubles.

"My mother will give you the rest. I don't have time."

I called her, and hurriedly explained what was happening. I pleaded with her to promise Vladimir she'd transfer money for the remaining amount. She reluctantly agreed, and Vladimir, perhaps realizing he wasn't going to find anyone else to buy the ticket in the two-and-a-half hours before the plane left, took her at her word. He passed over a plain envelope that held my ticket to freedom.

"Thank you, Vladimir," I said. "I'll let Ludmila know that you're doing well."

"Tell her to invite *me* next time!"

"I will for sure." I just wanted to run, run, run…

Now I had to get to the Pulkovo International Airport. The metro would not get me there in time, so my cousin Irina and her boyfriend came to the rescue. We made it in record time, swerving past cars and racing down streets, our horn blaring at anyone who dared get in our way.

"Please don't kill me!" I told them.

"Don't worry. You'll be all right."

"You can always come back home if you want," said Irina. "Maybe I can come and visit you."

"Please come to America. I wish you would come with me now. Please tell my friends that I am on my way to New York City and will be in touch soon."

It's funny how the most mundane things can leap to the top of one's mind in the midst of life's milestone moments. Here I was, flying off into the great unknown, and I was suddenly worried about who would return my library books, pay my phone bill, and finish my load of laundry. Irina put my mind at ease at least on that score by promising to call my friends, return my library books, and wash my clothes.

She gave me the name of a friend of hers who lived near San Francisco. Then, almost as an afterthought she said, "Here, take this medication with you. I heard pills are very expensive in America." She must have sensed that I was coming down with a sore throat. Thank heaven for afterthoughts.

It was fun to be a bit under the weather when I was little. I loved all the attention I received from my parents. They came home on time, and they let me watch TV and wander around in my flannel pajamas. They prepared bowls of chicken soup for me and let me stay home for a week when I had a cold or the flu. No antibiotics were prescribed. My father bought *gorchichniki* (sinapisms) and *banki* (glass cups used for fire cupping). My mother wrapped a cotton ball saturated with vodka or rubbing alcohol on the tip of medical scissors and lit it with matches inside the glass cup. She explained that oxygen would burn and create suction. I lay facedown on my pillow for at least fifteen minutes. *Gorchichniki* gave me a burning sensation; I guess it was from all the mustard on my chest and back. My mother wrapped a dry towel around my body and covered me in a heavy blanket to sweat.

"Irina," I asked my cousin, "can you call Mama and Papa tonight? Tell them that I love them and I'll be all right." I imagined the healing smell of mustard from my childhood.

"*Horosho* [good]," Irina said without much enthusiasm. She felt responsible for my decision.

She would be the one to explain to my family

and friends what had triggered me, at the age of only twenty-three, to leave my parents, White Pearl, my big family, and my country.

CHAPTER 3
ANXIETY AT THE AIRPORT

"Little things are indeed little, but to be
faithful in little things is a great thing."
—Mother Teresa

❦

The customs officer looked at me. "Get your
passport and ticket ready."

I looked nervously around at the other travelers.
What if this is a scam? What if Vladimir sold me a fake ticket?
One woman noticed that I was looking at her ticket.
She cautiously put it away in her purse. My ticket
showed my name, flight number, and the price it had
cost Vladimir. "Everything looks right to me," I said
to myself. Wait a minute! I looked again. My name
was handwritten in blue ink on the ticket. Would this

be a problem?

"Where are you going?" the customs officer asked me.

"New York," I replied, hoping to find out that I did have a "real" ticket. I looked back. My cousin was still waiting to see if I could get through the airport customs service.

My thoughts were racing like a fast-moving river. No, they were chattering and jumping like a monkey. I wanted them to stop and sit still. Then I turned to the same customs officer, who seemed to be friendly.

"I'm sorry," I said. "I just got the ticket. Can you tell me if it's real?" I was about to burst into tears.

"What do you mean by 'real'?"

"Well," I said quietly, "I bought this ticket from my friend Vladimir on the street. Can you please help me to get through the line?" I pleaded.

"Is Vladimir a *pharzovshik* [illegal trader on a black market]?" the man asked me.

"We were classmates."

"What else did you buy on the street?" He shook his head. "This generation is lost. Let me see your ticket, Kim. How many bags are you checking in?"

"This is all I have," I answered. I was embarrassed

that I only had a backpack.

He pointed to a counter. "Go and fill out the customs form," he said. "And don't lose your head."

I rushed over to the counter, my pen poised to fill out the required information. I looked more closely at the form. Suddenly I saw that all of the questions were in English. My stomach sank. I groaned in dismay.

The woman next to me must have sensed my distress. "What's wrong?" she asked in a kind voice.

"I can't figure out the form," I confessed.

And serendipity, good fortune, whatever you want to call it, once again came to my aid. This kind woman and her husband, from the Baltic States, helped me fill out the form. She spoke fluent English and, judging by her luggage and mink coat, also had good taste. They had leather suitcases unlike any I had ever seen.

She picked up my form. "What is the address of where you will be staying?" she asked.

I looked at her blankly and shook my head. "I have no idea."

She looked at me as if I were crazy. Perhaps I was.

I had one dollar in my pocket. I was about to get

on a plane, not knowing where I would end up or what I would do once I got there.

Perhaps sensing my growing alarm, she wrote her own New York City phone number on a piece of paper and gave it to me. "Don't worry," she said. "You can sit next to me on the plane." She patted me on the arm. "You'll figure it out once you get there."

That simple phrase has become my lifelong mantra. As fate would have it, however, I didn't get to sit next to my Good Samaritans on the plane. A moment later the customs agent, who had been searching their luggage, called over two armed guards and pointed to some money he had found in the lining of their suitcase. In January 1991, the average monthly salary of a doctor, teacher, or engineer was 267 rubles, or $5.68. The exchange rate was 47 rubles to the dollar. The black-market rate was 50 rubles to the dollar. Vladimir had charged me $900 for a round-trip ticket from Leningrad to New York City. I would have had to work for fifteen years to save that much. The kind lady who had helped me and her husband were "escorted" away. To this day, I wonder what happened to them.

The customs officer, having just caught someone trying to smuggle money, looked at my backpack suspiciously. "Where is your suitcase?" he demanded.

"I don't have one. This is all I'm taking," I said meekly, knowing my plane ride could disappear in an instant if he took a dislike to me.

"How much money are *you* taking with you?"

I took my lone wrinkled dollar out of my pocket and showed it to him.

"One dollar," he snorted with contempt. "You're going to end up homeless in New York. You can't even use a restroom for one dollar!"

"How do you know that?" I asked.

"My son moved to New York City in 1975," he said. "He's married, with children, and owns his own home. He's a very successful insurance broker."

What he was telling me echoed everything I'd heard about America. Money and houses. Money and houses. Everyone in America made lots of money and lived in a luxurious home.

"Maybe I should sell insurance when I get to New York?" I asked, trying to get on his good side.

Realizing that the people behind me were impatient to board and that there was nowhere I could have hidden anything anyway, the customs officer decided to stop giving me a hard time. He stamped my form and motioned me forward.

"You're okay."

"Thank you for your help."

"It's my job."

"Thank you again."

"Enough of thanking me. Please move forward. This flight is completely full."

Next I stood in a line to get on a yellow Ikarus (a bus manufactured in Budapest), which would take us to the airplane. Looking up, I saw thousands of stars like white beads all over the sky. It was maybe the darkest night of my life. My grandfather would say that a starry night meant a great day tomorrow.

My memories of my grandfather calmed me down. I loved sitting on the porch and stargazing with him. He taught me how to find the Great Bear and Orion. He always said, "There must be life on other planets."

Until New Year's of 1986, White Pearl's husband, my paternal grandfather Alexander Kim, had sent me gifts every year: boxes filled with oranges, pomegranates, raisins, walnuts, pistachios, and candies. That was the year "he went home to the heavens," as White Pearl would say. He was literate and opinionated and loved to discuss politics over dinner. His friend called him the "orator." My aunt said his temper was like a fire, easy to burn out, but he never got angry with me.

"He loved his grandchildren more than his own children," Grandmother told me. "He treated his children as adults, and he treated his grandchildren as children. When he lived in Korea, he and his older brother had a tutor to study Chinese. His father believed in discipline and good education for boys and girls. Learning Chinese required discipline, as it's a very difficult language. For each error, the tutor whipped his hands or back."

I loved my grandfather because he spent time with me and talked to me like I was his best friend. He bought me my first bicycle, a *shkolnik* or "school pupil" bike, and he gave me my first haircut.

I was five years old and still slightly too short to reach the pedals. I didn't want to wait to grow half an inch, however, so I stretched out my legs. It was a green two-wheeler with golden letters on it. Riding that bike became one of my favorite things to do…until one day when I was riding down a hill and lost control. My bike was going so fast that I couldn't even keep my feet on the pedals. And I didn't know how to use the brakes properly. At that moment it didn't matter. I was going way too fast! Bam! I ended up hitting a big oak tree. I flew up into the air then landed hard on the ground. That was my last ride that summer until my scraped knees and nose healed. My beloved bike was twisted out of shape.

I remember my first haircut...I was sitting on a high blue stool under the walnut tree in front of our house. My grandfather covered the ground with *Pravda*, one of the oldest Communist Party newspapers. My grandmother believed the old saying, "Hair on the ground, floor, or carpet is bad luck. Comb your hair and sweep it away."

That's why Grandfather decided to use the newspaper instead of sweeping. "Where did she read that?" he said to me. "It's pure nonsense. Maybe it's a women's thing."

"Why did you get a newspaper then?" I asked him.

"To keep this area clean." He cut out all the portraits of the members of the Politburo, or Central Committee of the Communist Party of the Soviet Union, out of respect for the country's leaders, before he used it for anything (newspapers were also a prime substitute for toilet paper from the 1960s to the '70s, due to shortages).

My hair was silky and very long, like White Pearl's.

But everyone was too busy to braid and wash my hair.

"It's too long," Grandfather kept saying. "Let's give you a nice haircut." One day I agreed to let him cut my hair. I hoped no one would tease me that I looked like a little old lady. My aunt Zoë always braided my long hair and rolled the braids around my ears.

"I don't like it," I told her. "I look like a girl from a very old book."

My grandfather had only one arm (he had been hit by a train and his left arm had been amputated), and the scissors he used on my hair were old and rusted. I could imagine how challenging it was for him to give me a nice haircut. He did his best.

"*Dedushka* [Grandfather]," I said, "I couldn't even cut the paper for my art project with these scissors because the blades were not sharp enough. I saw *Babushka* cutting dill for *borscht* the other day using the same scissors."

"Please don't move," he cautioned. "Let me cut your bob a little shorter." In no time at all, he handed me a round mirror and announced, "We're done. We're going to the photo atelier to take a family portrait."

"Grandfather, I look like a boy," I complained. "How can I take a photo looking like a boy?"

"Please don't worry. Your hair grows so fast. The purpose of the haircut is so that your hair doesn't cover your eyes and you can see better. You can read books and won't have to worry about losing your hairpins."

The only family portrait we ever took shows me when I was a little girl with my short bob.

My grandfather was always interested in politics, but he was expelled from the Communist Party in 1937 when Joseph Stalin began deporting Koreans from the Far East of Russia to Central Asia and the Caspian Sea area.

White Pearl told me, "Your grandfather believed that Communism would change the lives of people in Russia for the better. He was very angry when the deportation happened. Korean people were not trusted. After 1936, people were not only expelled from the party but many were executed or sent to prisons."

After gardening, reading was my grandfather's second passion. He took daily catnaps in his room, the smallest room in the back of the house where there were two single iron beds and a cabinet for his clothes. All of his documents were stored in a bag the color of wet asphalt.

My grandfather's room had a small window covered with newspapers—issues of *Pravda* that were faded yellow from the burning rays of the hot summer sun. He loved to keep his window open at night.

"Do you think that nature sleeps at night?" he once asked me.

"I don't know," I replied. "*Babushka* said that everyone must sleep at night."

"You should go outside and listen to the sounds at night. It's like an orchestra. Sometimes I don't recognize who made all these sounds. Night is beautiful."

As I began my journey, these memories brought me a great deal of comfort. Now I was hoping for a great day tomorrow in New York City. Ludmila had sent my invitation to me a year ago. She didn't even know that I had run into Vladimir and that he had sold me a ticket to New York. It was a direct flight from Leningrad to New York City. I'd be there in eleven hours. I couldn't wait to tell her about the innocent trip to a local bakery that changed my life in a way I could not possibly have imagined.

"Please take your seats," a steward announced as we boarded the plane. "Our flight is already delayed."

With a mixture of relief and disbelief, I walked down the aisle. It was my first time alone on a plane.

I made my way to the "business class," found my seat, stowed my backpack on the floor under the seat in front of me, and sank into the well-worn cushions.

Irina is probably home calling my mom and dad to say that I am now onboard the plane and on my way to New York, I thought. *I'll figure it out once I get there.*

I was on my way.

CHAPTER 4
THE FLIGHT TO
MY FUTURE

"I dwell in possibility..."
—Emily Dickinson

⁕

At first, I was too nervous to sleep on the plane.
The tension of the last few days and the constant
underlying fear that it could all fall apart at any
moment had accumulated into back pain that wouldn't
stop no matter how I shifted around in my small
space. Every seat on the plane was full, and it seemed
that every person in each of those seats was smoking
a foul-smelling cigarette. There were two sections on
this aircraft, "smoking" and "non-smoking." I think

my ticket had been originally sold to a businessman who probably smoked, ate caviar with a teaspoon, and drank vodka like water. Now I was sitting in his "smoking" first-class seat.

Drinks were served. Everyone around me was talking and getting to know each other, smoking and drinking. To put it briefly, they were having a good time. Not that I was complaining.

As I sat alone, I looked out the window at the black night and silently thanked every person who had contributed to my being on this plane. My grandmother, my many friends, my parents, the couple from the Baltic Sea, the man at the U.S. Consulate General who had impulsively decided to grant my visa when there were famous ballet dancers, professors, and musicians who'd had their applications turned down time after time. I was grateful to each and every one of them, even my old school buddy Vladimir, who had tried to take advantage of my desperation. I vowed to make good on their faith in me.

As we waited for the flight to take off, my mind drifted. I was back at my favorite place in the world, my grandparents' country house. It was a big house with an amazing orchard of apple, cherry, peach, and pear trees. Their garden grew fat with corn, squash, and pumpkins. I remembered Grandmother laughing one day and saying, "Hedgehogs love our tomatoes. One little baby is hiding under a cucumber leaf. He looks like my pincushion. Go and take a look."

"Life's interesting, my darling," my loving grandmother always told me. "Never, never give up your dreams, even if they seem impossible. Always have faith, even when no one is on your side. Give a smile, love, and goodwill to other people. Give what you want to receive. If you want more happiness, give that to others, too. You'll feel great about yourself. There's no end in our life—an end is only the beginning of something new. Life is a circle of love. When you do good things, good things come back to you. Let me touch your ears. See, you have a little grain of rice on your left ear. That means you are *tyagai iso* [lucky]. Anything you do, you do well." My grandmother touched my left ear to make sure "it" was still there. Ever since I can remember, I've had a small bump under the skin on my ear—a "lucky rice grain." You can't see it. I don't know what it is. But Grandmother always assured me that it would bring good fortune.

Sitting on the plane getting ready to fly to New York, I checked often to make sure the grain of lucky rice was on my left ear. *It's still there!*

Waiting for the plane to take off, I fell back into my memories of White Pearl and my family. "We all had chores to do on the farm," she had told me, "like preparing garlic for cooking." First, Grandmother would soak fresh bulbs of garlic in cold water for at least two or three hours so they would be easier to peel. Then she would grind the bulbs and mix them with coarse salt as a marinade. It always tasted fresh and could be stored in a cold place for a year. She used the same method to store chilies and fennel for winter.

I remembered watching my *babushka* sorting big cucumbers to her left and small ones to her right. "We will pickle cucumbers, tomatoes, green wild garlic, chili peppers, cabbage, and small watermelons," she said. "I will make *kvashenya kapusta* [sauerkraut]. It is the best *zakuska* [cold appetizer] when served with vodka to guests." She told me I could help her sort tomatoes. "We pickled almost everything for seven months of cold weather," she explained.

White Pearl made delicious *varenye* (jam) from fresh cherries, raspberries, and apricots with almonds and rhubarb. I climbed the tree with a small plastic bucket tied to my waist or draped from my neck to pick apricots. These homemade dried fruits were a delicious snack during my school breaks. As kids, we didn't eat many sweets. Chocolate and candies were pricey back in 1970s. Plombir (a brand of ice cream) was tasty, but it cost seven *kopeek*. Most of the time, I had bags filled with dried cherries, fried sunflower and pumpkin seeds.

White Pearl made rice with potatoes; the portion that was slightly burned on the bottom of her iron pot was called *kamachi*. I loved the crunchy, tasty, toasty crust of cooked rice. *Kamachi* was our homemade "chips."

I remembered that preparation for the long winter ahead always began in August. My grandmother sliced eggplants and dried them until the slices looked like French fries. I helped her to sort leaves of Napa cabbage and placed them on the table under a tree to keep them away from the sun. We covered them with cheesecloth to protect them from flies. We used dry cabbage leaves to make a soup called *seryagi*. In the afternoons, I picked chrysanthemums that we used to brew tea. Adults loved black tea from India. It came in a yellow package with an Indian man riding on the elephant. The package weighed only fifty grams. My grandfather poured leftover tea on the soil where red roses were planted. "It is good for the soil," he always said. "And it protects young rosebuds from bugs."

Starting in the fall, Grandmother piled fresh carrots, beets, and potatoes in a wooden box and covered them with sand, a technique that she had learned from her mother, Elena. The days were getting shorter and the nights were getting colder. The leaves and grass were changing color. Although the sun shined brightly in the daytime, the soil was too cold to walk on with my bare feet. We'd go to sleep on the outside porch, our bellies full, and wake up to the sounds of crickets chirping, chickens cackling, roosters crowing, and horses snuffling nearby. "Vegetables always stayed fresh until at least February," White Pearl used to say to me. Large cabbage buds with clusters of tender young leaves were wrapped in cheesecloth and hung on the wall for better air circulation, then stored for cooking. My grandparents stored at least ten forty-pound sacks of potatoes, carrots, and beets.

Every evening *Babushka* made dinner from scratch. She always cooked soup in a pot that was so big, it held at least a bucket of water. I can still taste her *borscht* ("red soup" or "beetroot soup"), and the classic Russian soup called *shchi.* I loved her *blini* (similar to French crêpes) and *piroshki* (turnovers) with mashed potatoes. Everyone knew that my grandmother was a great hostess and storyteller. During the summer, she usually served watermelon or ice-cold fruit compote with cherries or apricots for dessert. White Pearl didn't like to mix different berries or fruits. She boiled water with sugar and added fresh cherries. It simmered for half an hour and then chilled a few hours longer.

A second pot was also simmering on the stove for hours—it contained our laundry. The hot water helped to make the sheets whiter. Grandmother starched our bedding and grandfather's white shirts. He wore white shirts during the summer and dark ones during winter, even when he was working in the garden. I don't remember ever seeing him wearing a sweater—just a jacket, a hat, and his medal, the Order of the Badge of Honor, for his hard work during World War II. He had been in charge of organizing deliveries of wheat and rice to the Eastern front.

Grandmother hung the *kovry* (carpets) on the wooden fence, and then I helped her beat them with a stick to get rid of dust.

Teatime with my grandmother was one of my favorite parts of the day. It wasn't about the tea. I didn't like to drink black tea when I was five years old. What I loved was the time I spent with my *babushka*.

How can I ever forget the taste of tea from the Russian *samovar*? My grandmother's charcoal-burning *samovar*, a metal container to boil water for tea, held almost one whole bucket of water. It was our family tradition to finish a dinner with a cup of hot tea with milk and *ponchiki* (doughnuts), *bubliki* (rolls), and *kalachi* (Russian-style bagels). *Babushka's* tea was served in fragile white porcelain cups; the saucers had a floral design. Her sets of tumblers, mugs, saucers, teapots, and plates were stored in a *servant* (a glass-doored china cabinet). There was also a *kniznyi shkaff* (a glass-doored cabinet for books). These two cabinets looked alike and usually were supposed to be next to each other against the entire wall. They were also called *stenka* ("wall").

My chore was to wash the dishes after dinner and teatime. I added baking soda to warm water for washing, and I rinsed them twice with fresh water. Even as late as my escape from Leningrad in 1991, we didn't know about dishwashers.

My grandparents bought their first color TV in 1975. It took up half of the room. White Pearl loved to watch Indian movies. *Babushka* loved Indian love songs, traditional costumes, and dances. "I used to dance with your grandfather until I was completely exhausted," she used to tell me. My favorite film was

Zita i Gita (Seeta and Geeta). My grandmother and I laughed and cried watching this movie over and over again.

When it was bedtime, White Pearl always gave me a hug and said, "It's time to go to bed. I have to wake up early tomorrow. Good night."

"I'll water all the plants tomorrow," I always promised her. "Your red roses, pink hollyhocks, yellow pot marigolds, white peonies, and the violet garden phlox."

"Thank you, little helper!"

My cousin Irina and I spent all our summers at our grandparents' house.

At night I liked to try to scare Irina with horror stories that I either learned from other kids or made up. We often competed to tell the scariest tale.

"Do you think there is a ghost under our bed?" I whispered to my cousin. "I am not playing. I am serious."

"Of course not," she said. "We would see or hear the ghost. Don't you think?"

"Grandma told me they are invisible. You cannot see them. Sometimes they can be heard, though."

"I do not think they exist," she said. "I'm sleepy. *Spokoinoi nochi* [good night]." She disappeared under the blanket. "No more talking. It's time to sleep."

"We forgot to brush our teeth tonight," I reminded her, but then I too fell asleep.

The next morning we combed each other's hair into pigtails. We borrowed each other's dolls, dresses, and books. We also got into fights and made each other cry once in a while. One rule was that we couldn't scream or fight in front of our grandparents.

I was a tomboy and I loved to fish. Once, I cut a meter-long piece of my grandmother's brand-new cheesecloth to use as a fish net. My friends and I jumped into the river, and holding the corners tight we dragged the cloth against the current and caught tiny little fish. After playing in the water, I brought all the kids home, mostly boys, and we ate freshly made *piroshki*, a jar of apricot jam, and fruit compote, and we drank three liters of milk.

Then I encouraged everyone to leave the kitchen. "Let's go outside and jump rope." Suddenly, as we began to play, the kids let out terrifying screams and ran away, shouting, "Gypsies! Gypsies! The gypsies are coming. They steal children!"

I was left standing all alone in the middle of the street, when a gypsy woman came to me and asked, "Is anybody home?"

"No," I answered. She was tall, with shiny, jet-black hair down to her waist, a dark skirt with ruffles, a long tunic, and many bracelets on her wrists that jingled like bells.

"Can you bring me some food?" she asked me.

"*Horosho* [good]." I ran fast to get some.

Uh-oh, my grandmother's *piroshki* were all gone. I picked up a loaf of rye bread and ran back to her. "Here. This is all I have."

"That's all?"

My heart was pumping. I didn't know what else to give to a gypsy stranger. "Well," I said. "Let me go and see."

I grabbed hardboiled eggs, in fact, all of them—a dozen. I found cookies and candies that my grandmother had bought for a party. I put everything into a plastic bag and ran back to the gypsy woman.

"Here."

"Good," she said. "Let me ask you a question. Why didn't you run away from me like the others?"

"To be honest," I said, "I was afraid and tried to run, but I couldn't move."

She smiled. "Hmmm. Give me your palm." I obeyed and she looked at my hand for a long time.

"You have a big life," she said. "An interesting life. Your life is not easy. You have to work a lot. You have the palm of an old woman. You are an old soul. You will have a castle and people working for you."

I was so scared. *Why is she talking about souls? Does that mean death? I have been to so many funerals with my grandparents. Oh, gosh! Grandma, help! What does the soul mean? Is it like a ghost?*

The mystical gypsy disappeared, and I have never seen her or any other gypsy again since that day. When my grandmother came home that afternoon at four o'clock, I could hardly wait to tell her what had happened.

I lived in fear of gypsies and horses, ghosts and destiny. It was all new to a little girl like me. There was one other time that I had experienced fear like that— when I rode a horse. Chen Gym, the grandfather on my mother's side, tried to reassure me. He raised donkeys, cows, goats, pigs, rabbits, geese, and chickens on the farm, but he loved horses best. He believed that they were the most intelligent animals.

"Grandma," I said, "we ate all your *piroshki* and emptied all of the jars. I had kids over for *obed* [lunch]." Our lunch was usually from one o'clock to two o'clock in the afternoon. It would take me years to get used to eating lunch at noon in America. "Grandma," I continued, "I saw gypsies today!" I would not let White Pearl relax after her long day at the bazaar until I told her about my encounter.

"Wonderful," she said. "Ahhh. Gypsies... They are rare in our area. They travel and don't stay in one place. It's their way of life. They love music. You should give them food."

"Grandma, she told me about a castle and some lives I lived and that I have to work a lot."

"You are already working hard," White Pearl said. "You gather eggs in the chicken coop, wash the dishes, beat the carpets, and water the lilies and roses. What else did she tell you?"

"I am an old *dusha* [soul]. What is *dusha*? My knees were paralyzed from my fear today."

White Pearl gently patted me on my shoulder. "Just believe in the great life you will have. You are a creator of your own happiness and destiny," she said. "We have a spirit that guides us and protects us."

"I was so scared," I whispered. "Last night we talked about a ghost under our bed. And today a gypsy tells me about my soul. And destiny!"

"Do not worry," she affirmed. "You create your

own destiny." White Pearl looked into my eyes. "You will have a beautiful life."

"I love you so much." I hugged her tight with my small arms.

White Pearl laughed out loud. "Will you love me that much when I get old?"

My grandmother had borrowed my *chemodan* (a brown vinyl suitcase with rounded corners) to store the funeral clothing that she prepared for herself. I was only seven years old and scared to touch her "funeral" suitcase.

"Do not die, Grandma," I cried when I saw her funeral things. The suitcase was still in her house when I went to visit White Pearl in the fall of 2007.

White Pearl had assured me that if things didn't work out for me in America, I could always come back home. "You will never know the outcome until you take action," she told me. "You don't know what potential you have until you use your potential and God-given gifts."

As I sat on that Aeroflot plane waiting to take off for New York, I could still hear my *babushka*'s encouragement. "You are the firstborn," she said. "You turned out to be clever and adventurous. Your parents will always love you, no matter what." One day when we had chicken for supper, she told me, "If you eat chicken wings, you will fly away from your parents' home. If you eat chicken legs, you will run fast. If you eat the chicken neck, you will be beautiful like a white swan. This is for you," she said, giving me a chicken heart pierced with her fork. "Eat it and you will be lucky."

As a child, I always longed for the magic of holidays. I waited all year for the chance to make a wish for whatever I wanted. Frankly, I still do. I wish the spirit of New Year's would last throughout our lives. Once a year, on the long night of New Year's Eve, I could go to bed at the time I would normally wake up to go to school. Our winter *kanikuly* (winter recess) lasted more than two weeks, and school resumed on January 15, after my birthday on January 11. I could recall the fresh green scent of the *elka* (Christmas tree) and how my mother made crunchy waffles stuffed with condensed milk. I also enjoyed having free time to take photography classes, read my favorite books, play with our neighbors' kids, and get plenty of sleep.

I enrolled at our local library when I was seven years old and my mother took me there every week to borrow three books to read for the next week. For ten years, she recorded all the books I had read since the first grade on a long scroll. "You have read *Thumbelina, The Princess and the Pea, The Snow Queen, Pippi Longstocking,* and *Moomintrolls,*" my mother said. She carefully marked each book down on the list. "We have a long way to go. You are such a good reader. You're like your father."

"And *Babushka* and my grandfather, too," I corrected her.

"Yes," she agreed. "You are absolutely right."

My mother was the first in her family to go to medical college in Kzyl-Orda. Then she moved to the city of Ivanovo, near Moscow, to be closer to my father who applied to the Leningrad Institute of Civil Engineering. His sister, Ludmila, got married in Leningrad in 1960 and had her first child there.

My mother had seven siblings: five sisters and two brothers. She was the oldest child and was always busy watching the other kids. My maternal grandmother, Natasha, would start milking cows at five o'clock in the morning and then get ready to work in the kitchen at the local hospital. On April 20, 1965, my grandmother received the *Orden Materinskya Slava*, Level 3 (Order of Maternal Glory, Level 3) for having seven children, and on May 25, 1968, she received the Order of Maternal Glory, Level 2, for having her eighth child. Grandmother Natasha also had a child who died at the age of twelve months and another who was stillborn. If those children had lived, she would have been eligible for the Order of Maternal Glory, Level 1, for having nine children, or the *Mat Geroinya* (Order of Mother Heroine) for having ten children.

Natasha's Order of Maternal Glory, Level 2, established on July 8, 1944, to reward mothers, is right here on my desk as I write this book. On the front is an enamel ribbon shaped like a knot. The ribbon is white with a blue stripe in the center. On the left of the badge is the figure of a mother holding a child, and behind them is the Red Flag with the Cyrillic inscription *Materinskaya Slava* (Maternal Glory) over the Roman numeral II, designating the level of the reward. At the bottom is the hammer and sickle.

My mother's family lived in the Far East of Russia, where White Pearl's parents had emigrated from Korea. My mother's father, Chen Gym, always carried sugar cubes in his black *vatnik* (quilted jacket).

"Grandfather, your *vatnik* is heavy," I complained when he asked me to hold it. "I can't hold it for you."

"Hmm," he said. "I didn't think of that. But it keeps me warm."

"Your pockets are sticky from the sugar cubes," I complained again. "Did you notice that?"

"I keep those for *Zarya* [Dawn]," he said, pointing at his favorite horse. "She has a sweet tooth, like you."

"Strange," I said. "I was giving her a bucket of pears and a bucket of apples. I think she liked them very much. And she liked sunflowers seeds. Grandfather, I don't eat many sweets."

"Horses can feel fear," he warned me one day as I was trying to climb on the back of a horse. My young mind couldn't wrap itself around that. I was afraid to ride, and I didn't see how a horse's sensing fear could be a sign of intelligence. One warm day, I watched *Zarya* grazing in the field and decided it was time to get over my fear. I got on her back with a help of my cousin, and she placidly walked around. *Hmm*, I said to myself. *Nothing to fear about that.* The next day, we graduated to a trot. I managed to stay on. It was fun bouncing up and down on her broad back. The next day, we cantered, and I remembered my hair flying out behind me as I experienced the most exquisite feeling of freedom. On a horse, you can explore. Even though I was five years old, I felt tall and strong. *Zarya* taught me that potential is released and realized only when you decide to overcome your fear.

I went to sleep on the porch that night with a wide smile on my face as I remembered the lesson I learned while riding *Zarya*. I woke up to the sound of the crickets and chickens...but, wait a minute. That noise wasn't crickets or chickens or anything outdoors. What was that noise?

It was the sound of someone clicking shut an overhead bin. I opened my eyes. I had been dreaming of home. I wasn't on my grandparents' porch; I was on a plane. I looked out the window. It was light. I could see the ocean—the ocean!—below me. The captain announced on the intercom that we would be landing at John F. Kennedy International Airport in twenty minutes.

This was not a dream. It was really happening!

CHAPTER 5
WELCOME TO AMERICA.
NOW WHAT?

"To travel hopefully is a better thing
than to arrive."

—Robert Louis Stevenson

᧬

Eight o'clock in the morning on Wednesday,
December 18, 1991, John F. Kennedy International
Airport—*Welcome to America!*

I walked off the plane and into mass confusion. It
was the holiday season, and the airport was bustling
with activity—Christmas trees, crying babies, travelers
with brightly wrapped gifts rushing to catch their
flights. Lines for food. Reunions. Leave-takings.

People running into each other's arms. (This was before 9/11, when those without tickets could still go to the gate with their loved ones.)

I stood in the midst of the nonstop motion, people bumping me as they rushed past. It seemed that everyone but me knew where to go. I finally spied an empty chair and claimed it. I sat down, hugging my backpack to my chest. I had no idea what to do next. The sounds of a language I didn't understand gave me a headache. People talked so fast that I couldn't even catch a sound I recognized. My head was spinning. I felt dizzy. How was I going to contact Ludmila? I couldn't read any of the signs. Everything was in English. But what did I expect? I didn't know whom to ask for help or even how to ask. And, besides, no one would understand me anyway.

The magnitude of what I'd done, leaving home without a plan, without a clue, suddenly hit me. I sat there, almost in a state of shock, for eight hours. A rather handsome young man sitting in the opposite row of chairs kept glancing in my direction. He looked my age or slightly older; maybe he was a student. He was wearing a sweatshirt and jean jacket and sneakers. He was very tall. Maybe he played tennis or football. His shoulders were broad and his eyes were kind. He must have been wondering why I'd been sitting there so long. Finally, he approached and said something. When I answered in Russian, his eyebrows rose in surprise. He said something else. I answered in German. "No," he said to me, shaking his head. I showed him the invitation from Ludmila and pointed to her phone number. He nodded his head to indicate he understood, mimed holding a phone to his ear, and then pointed to himself. The international language of gesturing seemed to be working for us. I nodded enthusiastically. He motioned for me to wait there, held up two fingers and "walked" them to show me he would search for a phone and call my friend. I offered him my only dollar. He not only returned my only dollar but gave me a few coins besides.

Then he disappeared. He came back a few minutes later, a perplexed expression on his face. He kept saying, "Canada." As I would eventually learn, my friend Ludmila had given up on me when she didn't hear back. She had moved to Canada. I still don't know what happened to her. We have not seen or talked to each other since.

But I understood about Canada. It sounded very similar in Russian. My father and I watched all the hockey games. His favorite players were Valery

Kharlamov and his teammate of many years, goaltender Vladislav Tretiak. They were my favorite players, too. My father and I had spent all his free time together. He took me to the May Day parade every year and dressed me in a red barrette, a red coat, and white pants. We went on fishing trips and camping together. He taught me how to ski and ice skate, which I was good at and enjoyed tremendously.

So here I was in America. What could I do? The only option I had was to go to California to visit my friend Nina's cousin Galina, whom I'd never met in my life. I showed the kind stranger Nina's letter asking Galina to help me. I pointed to San Francisco on my map. He shook his head and pointed on the map to New York City. I nodded my head several times to let him know I knew we were in New York and that San Francisco was across the country. Then I borrowed his pen and drew a plane and a question mark on the back of the envelope and pointed at the San Francisco sign again.

The young man went over and talked to the gate agent for a moment. He jotted something on the envelope, and then came back and gave it to me. It had "$1,300" written on it. I pulled out my one dollar and showed it to him. He just looked at me. Then I had a brainstorm. I grabbed the envelope from him, turned it over, and drew a bus. He nodded as if this was a possibility and disappeared again, longer this time. He returned with a more hopeful look and showed me what was written on the envelope: "$168." With a rueful smile, I showed him my one dollar again.

He was stumped. He plopped down in the chair next to me to mull this over. After a moment, he seemed to make up his mind. He pointed to the "$168" and then tapped himself on the chest. He would buy my bus ticket for me! He stood up and gestured for me to follow him. I picked up my backpack, and we went out into the cold to catch the subway to the Greyhound Bus Terminal in New York City.

I had my first look at New York. What did I see? My new world was noisy and fast. Didn't anyone ever slow down in America? I was exhausted. I hadn't had anything to eat or drink since I'd arrived. I had spent at least eight hours sitting in the terminal. At that moment, what I wanted more than anything else was to drink a glass of water, brush my teeth, and lie down in a bed and sleep. But even if I had money, I couldn't even read the prices for a cup of coffee or a muffin. I was surprised to see people buying bottles of water. I had drunk tap water all my life. I thought, *Someone is selling water? What a businessperson!* I had heard so many times that America is the land of opportunity. Now, on my first day in America, I had witnessed it with my own eyes.

Since then, many people have asked what my first glimpse of New York City was like. I tell them that despite having arrived at the destination of my dreams, I didn't dare look around very much. It was loud and cold, and I was so afraid of losing my "guide" that I just stayed glued to his side. The subway ride was a blur, although as soon as we walked into the Greyhound Bus Station, it felt and looked different.

"Leningrad's subway is made from marble and bronze. And New York's subway is old and dirty," Ludmila had once told me. I saw what she meant.

People at the airport had been dressed up, many wearing coats and hats of mink, sable, chinchilla. (This was before wearing fur was politically incorrect.) It had almost looked like home—well, that is, if people spoke English in Russia.

But here? Here in the bus station, it was a crowded cacophony of noises and smells—not all of them pleasant—and people were definitely not dressed up. My newfound friend went to the window, bought my ticket, and took me to Door 8. He indicated that I was to stay right there because this was where my bus would be. Then, without any fanfare, my white knight gave me a hug and a small wave good-bye. I never saw him again. I never even knew his name.

What can I say? It was a miracle. What were the odds of another Good Samaritan going out of his way to help a lost-looking young Korean woman from Russia who couldn't speak English? What motivated this young man to extend himself to me? To buy my ticket, to shepherd me through the maze of the New York subway? To get me to the bus station and make sure I was safely on my way?

Some people who have heard my story are curious as to why I trusted him. They seem to think I should have been more suspicious. After all, this was New York City. They're surprised to discover that I so willingly followed a stranger out of the airport and onto the subway.

The thought that this young man might have intended to harm me never entered my mind. He was so clearly trying to help. Even without a common language, we had a common bond. I often think of the kindness of this stranger and try to repay him every chance I get by extending myself to others who might be in need.

Even though the bus to San Francisco wasn't scheduled to leave for several hours, I didn't budge from my spot by the designated door. When the bus finally drove up, I was the first one on. It didn't look like the buses we had at home. It was big and had tinted windows and soft seats. Little did I know that I was embarking upon a trip that would last three days, three hours, and five minutes, with stops in forty-six cities and few bathroom visits. I didn't even know that the lavatory was a few seats behind me. (To be honest, I couldn't even imagine having a restroom on a bus.)

There were students on the bus. They offered me something to eat and drink, though I didn't accept it. I had four hour-long stops and was able to go in to the bus terminals, use their restrooms, and drink water from the water fountains. People were going home to celebrate Christmas with their families.

I remembered how one of our neighbors at home would be wearing a costume of *Ded Moroz* ("Grandfather Frost," similar to Santa Claus) and carrying a big sack filled with candies, cookies, *ledenzy* (popsicles) shaped like roosters, and tangerines. I would not be there this year.

Ded Moroz always asked me to read my favorite *stishok* (poem) in order to receive a gift. I used to recite poems of my choice every day until I felt satisfied with my performance. I believed that he was the one who froze rivers and covered the land with snow. I also believed he was the same age as my grandfather and lived in Siberia. He always traveled with his granddaughter, *Snegurochka* (the snow maiden), who wore a traditional long blue Russian costume and a white hat. Her golden-colored braids fell to just below her waist.

I made big snowflakes from white sheets of paper. They were so big we could see them on the windows from a block away. My mother didn't let me use glue on the glass. Instead, I used face soap. I also made snowflakes using small cotton balls attached to a thread and hung them all over the windows and the ceiling in our apartment. We kept all of the ornaments up until my birthday. I used watercolor paint to draw *Ded Moroz* and *Snegurochka* on the window. I had studied drawing and painting with a passion from the first grade through the eighth grade, and I used any occasion to practice.

On January 6, we had friends over for the Russian Orthodox Christmas dinner. My mother's traditions included *lepit pelmeni* (to shape dumplings), which reminded me of Chinese dumplings, but with two corners stuck together. She wrapped minced pork with onions in round, thin dough and cooked the dumplings for a few minutes until they floated. She served them with sour cream on the side. I used to make one "lucky" *pelmeni* with a coin inside.

"Someone could break a tooth on that coin," my mother said. "I would use a garlic or red hot chili instead." (My family loved spicy food.)

Now in 1991, I would be spending my New Year alone. I wondered, who would help my mother make at least a hundred *pelmeni*? Who would bake a cake? Who would send holiday cards to all our relatives? Despite the fact I had no place to stay and no one waiting for me, and I was too embarrassed to accept food on the bus, I was on my way to California. I still feel fortunate every time I see a Greyhound bus.

CHAPTER 6
THE KINDNESS OF
STRANGERS

"Courage is doing what you're afraid
to do. There can be no courage unless
you're scared."

—Eddie Rickenbacker

I was exhausted and famished when I finally got off the bus in San Francisco. Ideally, this cross-country bus trip would have been an opportunity to see America up close out the window, a chance to see the rolling hills, the bustling cities, the wheat-filled plains, the quintessential small towns, the Rockies, and the rest of the things that make America famous. But I didn't dare step off the bus at the forty-six (yes, I counted them) fifteen-minute stops to drop off and board passengers. Not knowing English, I was terrified to venture into the terminals on such quick stops to try to find the restrooms. What if I returned and found that my "home away from home" had left without me? I couldn't risk it. So I stayed put, growing weaker and sicker by the hour. I was drifting farther and farther away from my sweet home in Russia.

I arrived in San Francisco at 11 p.m., December 22, 1991, three days before Christmas. The bus driver woke me up, pointing to the empty seats and the dark night outside. He helped me get my backpack. Although I knew that it was time to leave the bus, I was surprisingly reluctant to do so. Despite feeling miserable and sick from dehydration, I felt that the bus represented some safety and familiarity. Everyone else had disembarked, but I still sat there, unable, unwilling to move.

The bus driver walked back to my seat; he put his hand on my shoulder, and looked into my eyes. "San Francisco," he said, and pointed to the door. I saw that I was the only one left in the back of the bus.

"Sacramento?" I asked and showed him Nina's letter with an address in Sacramento.

"No." He showed me his watch and pointed to the time.

I realized that we had passed Sacramento two and a half hours ago.

"*Spasibo* [thank you]," I told him. *How could I have fallen asleep just before Sacramento?* I was muttering at myself. *I just can't believe myself!*

"*Spasibo*," the bus driver repeated after me with a smile.

So I picked up my backpack and stepped off the bus. It was the scariest night of my life. I have been afraid of darkness since I was a little girl. The night was mysterious to me.

Unlike the busy New York bus terminal, the San Francisco terminal was deserted. I needed to call Galina in Sacramento. (Later I learned from a family with whom I stayed for a short time that Galina had gotten married and moved to Las Vegas three months earlier. Apparently, they had called her mother, who also lived in Sacramento, and told her about me, but her mother didn't want a stranger in her house. That I understood.) Now I started to walk outside, but one look around quickly convinced me that Mission Street was no place to be at night. I retreated back inside the terminal and curled up on a hard bench, waiting for the unknown. I knew that ultimately I had to face reality. I also had to find something to eat. So I walked outside again, not sure of what awaited me.

After walking only a few blocks, I was deep in what I would later learn was the Tenderloin District. The drunks, the hookers, and the street people all looked at me speculatively. I avoided eye contact. I did my best not to challenge anyone and tried not to look like an easy mark. It didn't work. A homeless man, perhaps sensing how scared I was, grabbed my backpack and tried to yank it off my shoulder. With my fur coat, warm boots, mittens, and scarf, I must have looked like I had just arrived from Alaska. My mother had knitted my thick mittens from goat yarn. I was sure he had never seen such things before. Maybe he needed my mittens more than I did. I was worried about my little phone book with Galina's address in it. If I lost that contact, I was in big trouble. I opened my mouth to scream. Nothing came out. I tried again to call for help. Not even a squeak. My vocal cords had given out.

Having had nothing to eat and little to drink for three days, I was so dehydrated I had no voice left, no strength to fight back. A young man had called the police when he saw that I was being attacked. Fortunately, before the homeless man could take off with my backpack, a police car pulled up to the curb and two police officers jumped out. The homeless man headed off in the other direction as fast as his shuffling feet could take him.

As one of the police officers chased him, the other one hovered over me. "Passport?" he asked.

At least, I think that's what he asked. It sounded like passport in Russian. He was speaking English, which was, as they say, Greek to me.

Next, he asked my name (I guess). When I answered in Russian, he realized this was going to be a little more complicated than he had anticipated. I was on the verge of fainting, and so, not knowing what else to do, they piled me into the back of the police car and took me to the local station. At this point, I was past caring. This wasn't exactly what I had in mind for my first day in San Francisco, but it sure beat getting mugged.

The first thing they did was feed me. Warmed-up noodle soup never tasted so yummy. I drank glass after glass of water. The two police officers watched in amazement as I gobbled down everything they put in front of me. Only after I had been fortified with food did they start asking more questions.

Not knowing what else to do, I pulled my red Russian passport out of my backpack and showed it to them. Their eyes lit up and they exclaimed in unison, "Stolichnaya!"

I smiled. "*Da* [yes], Stolichnaya." It was as if we were playing a word association game. To them, Russia equaled the famous vodka, Stolichnaya. What they may not have known was that in my country you wouldn't think of going to someone's house without bringing along a gift bottle of vodka. I wish that I could have given these two officers a bottle of Stolichnaya for coming to my rescue.

They disappeared for a while. I didn't know it, but they were trying to find someone who spoke Russian. They finally located someone who was not only familiar with the language, but who knew someone else who would take me in until I could get on my feet.

I found out that San Francisco has the second-largest Russian-American population after New York City. I heard the Russian language everywhere I went in San Francisco. I was first referred to Elvira, an older woman who lived in a low-income project. She suggested I take a taxi over to her place. The taxi ride from the bus terminal to her apartment building cost eight dollars, which she paid when I arrived. I stayed with her for a few weeks.

Elvira helped me to find an immigration attorney. She was teaching Russian to John, an attorney in a small town near San Francisco. Elvira talked to him and he promised to find a lawyer for me. John called us the same day and gave us the phone number for an immigration attorney, Terry. Elvira and I scheduled an appointment with her and when we met, Terry agreed to take my case and help me become a U.S. citizen.

After a few weeks of staying with Elvira, I was referred to another Russian lady. She considered herself a *White Russian*. White Russian? I felt like I was in a movie. I had never seen a White Russian, only read about them in history books. White Russians were either assassinated by Bolsheviks or fled from Russia when my grandmother was a little girl.

Anastasia, the White Russian lady, had escaped from St. Petersburg with her mother just after the October Revolution of 1917. They had settled in Paris, where she became an artist and married a French art dealer. Her first language was French, as most of the noble families in czarist Russia spoke French. She'd had French tutors, governesses, and a nanny who taught her Russian. Russian was her second language. I called her "Madame."

"There were two groups in Russia," she would explain. "Red and White." Members of the *Belaya Armiya* (White Army), whose military arm opposed the Bolsheviks after the October Revolution on October 25, 1917, in Petrograd (St. Petersburg today), fought against the Red Army during the Russian Civil War.

Anastasia lived in the neighborhood in San Francisco called Pacific Heights. Her Victorian house had a nice garden with magnolia and cherry trees, and was conveniently located close to the park and a bookstore down the street. Her living room was filled with black-and-white photos of her family, and a grand piano which took up half of the living room.

Anastasia was stunning for her age. Blond curly hair, small stature, well dressed. She reminded me of a Russian ballerina from *Swan Lake.* A woman came to her house every Saturday to style her hair, and she also had a French manicure done every week. Anastasia meticulously counted calories and never gained an ounce of weight. Her favorite thing was a cup of black coffee and a slice of a *rulet* (pie) with honey and poppy seeds from a local bakery owned by Russians, on Geary Street in the Richmond District.

"That's enough calories for a day," she would say after the coffee and pie.

I drank coffee with three spoons of sugar until Anastasia said to me, "Honey, that is too much sugar for you."

"I need sugar," I always told her. "My dad and I always use two teaspoons of sugar per cup."

"For what?" she asked.

"I am thinking a lot lately. My brain burns tons of calories a day."

"We all think a lot," she continued. "That's why we have brains."

Soon Anastasia was my new employer. I was making money by reading books to her. I didn't last too long, though, because she would not let me go outside and meet other people.

"No strangers in my house," she told me.

One night I was reading to her from a book and she was snoring again. I couldn't take it anymore. I dropped *War and Peace* on the floor.

Her eyes opened immediately. "Why did you stop? Continue. I am paying you good money. Five dollars a night. Continue."

"If you want me to read, you should listen to the story."

"Get out of my house!" she exclaimed.

"It's night outside, Madame. Can I leave tomorrow morning?"

"Get out right now, or I am going to call the police."

I was on the street again. I started walking down Fillmore Street, stunned and anxious. Everything was closed except a bar. I went inside, where it was dark and filled with smoke.

"What would you like to drink?" the young man behind the bar asked me.

I pulled out a five-dollar bill, looked at it, and put it back in my pocket. "No," I replied.

"Where are you from?" he asked.

Without saying a word, I showed him my red Russian passport. I was thinking how it had happened that I was on the street again.

"Gorbachev," he said, smiling at me. Then he pointed to the clock on the wall, and I knew I had to leave soon. It was past eleven o'clock. I was explaining that I needed a place to stay when his partner came in and they hugged and kissed each other. At that point, I fainted. I had never seen two men kissing each other. In Russia, homosexuals were considered to be criminals and were persecuted.

Apparently someone splashed cold water over my face to help me regain consciousness. My only clean T-shirt was wet! When I opened my eyes, I saw their smiling faces.

The three of us walked to their apartment. They give me a blanket, a big pillow, and a clean white T-shirt with a sign in English that I could not read. I would sleep on a couch. I crawled under the blanket and closed my eyes.

I was grateful for their kindness, and I didn't notice when I fell asleep. The smell of coffee woke me up.

"Good morning," I greeted them first.

"Good morning, breakfast is ready," they said to me.

"Thank you very much." I took a plate of strawberries, toast with peanut butter, and a big mug of coffee. After I finished my meal, I decided to clean all the dishes.

"No, thank you," said Freddy. "Take whatever you want." He opened the refrigerator for me.

"We are going to Africa! And you can stay here for free," they said, surprising me.

I understood that they had to go to Africa (Africa

in English sounded like it did in Russian).

"Good," I responded. It was one of the words that I learned and used frequently.

They wrote, "30 days gone."

I understood that they would be in Africa for thirty days. Freddy gave me three keys and explained that one was for the front door to their building and two for their apartment. Also, a young guy would come every Friday to clean the apartment while they were in Africa.

How can you leave a house to a stranger? I wondered. *How can you let a stranger stay at your house and go to Africa?*

The next day, Freddy showed me the Korean Center, which was located two blocks from their apartment building. I walked there to see if it had a library where I could borrow books. Yes, indeed, there was a small library on the second floor. However, most of the books were written in Korean. The Korean Center offered ESL (English as a second language) classes to the public, especially to low-income people. I had *no* income, so I was very qualified. (I do not remember the fee, but it was around fifteen dollars for a three-month class.) At least I learned my ABCs and how to spell my last name: "Kei-ai-em."

I decided to call myself Lana instead of Svetlana because it was easier to spell. It felt great to be able to spell my name. The ESL class had a large group of students, most of them new to America. There were Russians, Ukrainians, and Jews. I enjoyed learning English. The teacher's name was Terry. Terry taught English at City College and was working on his Ph.D. at the same time.

Fundamentals of English Grammar by Betty S. Azar became my Bible as I religiously studied English every day. I still spoke broken English, pronouncing vegetables as VEGI-TABLES and strawberries as STRAW-BERRIES (two words). I got used to drawing things and pointing at words in the Russian-English Dictionary. I would also listen to people's conversations and write down a few words, then come home and find them in a dictionary that my mother had given me as a gift the year before.

I had started studying German at the age of eleven and had been told that if I spoke one foreign language, it would be easier to learn another. But even though I spoke both Russian and German, English was still very challenging. One day, however, I woke up from a dream in which I spoke fluent English! *Oh, well,* I told myself, *it was just in my dream.* I brushed my teeth, dressed, made a cup of instant coffee with two spoons of sugar, grabbed my books, and ran outside to practice the words I had learned the night before. But that day was a turning point. My English became more fluent when I began to dream in English. When I talked to myself, I talked in English, bad or good, it didn't matter. It was important for me to get rid of my fear not only of speaking English but also of bad English. I did not want to be embarrassed.

Terry, my teacher at the Korean Center, gave me some practical advice and cheered me up. "Take it easy," he said. "People won't dislike you if you make a mistake. Just have fun. Learning is a process. You have to practice a lot. The core of discipline is consistency. Be consistent in your studies. Be patient." Then he paid me an enormous compliment. "I can't imagine myself going to Russia with one dollar, not speaking Russian, and having no place to stay. You are doing a great job!"

Yes, it sounded very simple, but it was challenging to learn English. His words of encouragement were exactly what I needed at that time. Occasionally, Russian words still jumped out of my mouth from nowhere, like *da* instead of yes, or *nyet* instead of no.

I thought back to my early life and how a love for learning was instilled in me by my grandparents and later, my parents. I was raised by my grandparents because my father was in medical school and could not afford to rent a bigger apartment and raise a child. My grandparents were also taking care of my cousin Irina, who was four years older than me, for the same reason, since her parents were both students and could not afford to raise her.

In 1974, my grandfather said to me, "You will be going back to your parents." He was holding a letter from my father. "You are like a daughter to me. I will miss you terribly."

"No," I cried. "I don't want to leave you and *Babushka*. I am almost six years old. I have lived with you since I was one and a half."

"Well," he continued, "you need to go to a good school and be with your parents." He was trying to convince me.

"How can I stay in touch with you? We don't even have telephones."

"Simple," he said. "I am going to teach you how to write letters. I will give you a stack of envelopes and some postage stamps before you leave. In fact, we should go to the post office together. I will show you where to post a letter and how it all works. It is simple." He gave me his pen. "I wrote down our address for you. The number of the house goes first, then the street name, city, *index* [the Russian equivalent of a ZIP code], and my name."

"But I don't know my home number, street name, city, and *index*," I repeated back to him, afraid to miss anything.

"Pay attention," he said. "If you miss any of that information, it will be difficult for the *pochtalyon* [postman] to find me or Grandmother."

My grandfather taught me how to write letters, including official letters. Grandfather and I wrote to each other religiously about weather, books, food, flowers, birds, our dog Tuzik, our neighbor's cat Vasiliy, and my cousins. My grandfather would usually write four-page letters:

> *I bought twenty yellow and brown chicks. You should see them. A few of them got sick. I fed them fresh hardboiled eggs and penicillin. They easily get cold. I keep them in our summerhouse. The neighbor's cat was wandering around. I'm going to the farmers' market to buy a cage for the chickens to protect them from the cat. Love, your grandfather.*

I wrote back one page but it took me years to practice how to write three-page letters like my grandfather did:

> *Dear Grandfather, I miss you very much. I can't wait until summer comes so I can see you and Grandma. I am reading many interesting books but my favorites are* The Adventures of Tom Sawyer *and* Robinson Crusoe. *My parents are barely home. They work very hard. I called my dad at work and told him that I was bored. His response was that I should use my imagination and read a good book. Indeed, that good book is about Dr. Schliemann and his work on the discovery of Troy. You will enjoy this book. My teacher told me to study German at the university. I sent a letter to Moscow State Institute of International Relations. It's a public university affiliated with the Ministry of Foreign Affairs in Russia. I have a secret! My father wrote my mother love letters that are hidden in my mother's* shkaff [a mirrored wardrobe—apartments in Russia didn't have closets].

My grandfather's letters were a breath of fresh air for me. I read them every day until the next letter arrived.

A few months later I received a letter from the

Moscow State Institute of International Relations (MGIMO). They thanked me for my letter. How many did they get from fifteen-year-old girls who are interested in their programs? And they explained that they gave preference to members of the Communist Party, individuals who had served in the army for at least two years. Also, applicants needed a recommendation letter from local officials.

At that time, I still had two years of high school left. What was my next choice? What did my future look like? I was interested in economics, languages, literature, art, and photography. I had a private tutor from the world-renowned *Pushkinskiy Dom* (the Institute of Russian Literature) for three years to study Russian and writing.

My tutor's specialty was eighteenth- and nineteenth-century Russian literature. We met at his house every week. I was constantly reading and writing essays. I read the works of Pushkin, Gogol, Dostoevsky, and Turgenev.

A written essay was one of the enrollment requirements. If you failed the written essay, you were not able to take the rest of the tests. We could apply only to one college or university at a time. The age limit for higher education was thirty-five.

Writing an essay for six hours was the most challenging exam that applicants had to face. On the day of the first exam, about a thousand applicants sat in one big auditorium to write their essays. We had three topics to choose from and six hours to write in a descriptive style, with one optional thirty-minute break. Unlike students in America, we didn't have the luxury of test prep books or any test practices. All the applicants *(abiturients)* had three oral exams. We were asked to pick one exam ticket, the size of an index card, with two questions. Each applicant would have thirty minutes to prepare his or her presentation.

My cousin Irina was accepted at the First Medical Institute in Leningrad. I was told to follow her steps, but instead I applied to and was accepted at Leningrad State University (LGU), which made my grandparents and parents proud of me.

CHAPTER 7
TALKING TO THE ANIMALS: LEARNING ENGLISH AT THE SAN FRANCISCO ZOO

"We are made to persist. That's how we find out who we are."

—Tobias Wolff

❦

I was still carrying Nina's letter with me. I believed that one day I would meet her cousin, Galina, and, sure enough, a few months after I arrived in San Francisco, Galina and her husband came to meet me. They gave me almost $400. That meeting was thanks to a man I had asked to call Galina at her job. I could not believe that he had found her, but he told me that she would come to San Francisco from Las Vegas on her next business trip. And she did.

I was very happy to meet Galina. I was also glad I hadn't lost Nina's letter. "I have a letter from your cousin for you," I said as I handed it to her.

"Thank you," she said. She didn't speak Russian, except for a few words that even the police officers who rescued me after I got off the Greyhound bus knew.

"Nina feels much better, not sick anymore," I tried to say in English. Galina had invited Nina to stay in her house in Spain after having surgery in Moscow, where Nina's only daughter lived. Nina and her husband, an army colonel, were divorced.

When she finished reading the letter, Galina pulled her checkbook out of her purse and wrote me a check. It was hard to believe that this piece of paper was real *dengi* (money). We didn't have checks in Russia, only cash. Everything—your gas and electric bills, your telephone and water bills—had to be paid in cash at your local office.

"I hope this helps," she said as she handed the check to me. "This is from my husband Jim and me. I wish I could be more helpful. Don't lose this check. It's money for you."

"No," I told her. "I can't accept this."

"Nina asked me in her letter to help you," she replied. "She worries about you. She said that you come from a good family. This is on behalf of Nina."

Now I accepted the check. "Thank you. But I will need your address so I can send your money back when I get a job."

"Please don't worry about that. Sorry, we have to go now."

Our meeting lasted about fifteen minutes. Galina's husband did not say a word beyond his greetings and his last words, "Good-bye."

My days at that time were mine to go where I wanted, when I wanted, and the way I wanted. It's hard to express what it was like to have the freedom to explore a fascinating city in which everything I saw was new. One day I took the number 47 bus to the San Francisco Zoo. "Lions, tigers, and elephants, oh my!" I said aloud. When I saw an animal I didn't recognize, I wandered over to the placard to see if I could read the name. To my surprise and delight, the origin of the name was in Latin. "Eureka!" I shouted.

I can read Latin. In fact, I was able to translate part of the description of this mysterious animal. I recognized several of the words. Lion, *Panthera leo* in Latin and *lev* in Russian; giraffe, *Giraffa camelopardis,* sounded similar to the Russian, *zhirav.* Hmmm.

I went to the next animal enclosure. It was an elephant. No mistaking that. The description of its native habitat, preferred food source, and history had several words that I could now decipher. I was finally on to something. I pulled out my ever-present notebook and started copying down the names of the animals I knew. *That's a zebra. There's a giraffe. Those are monkeys. So that must be how you spell zebra, giraffe, and monkey in English.* I wrote down other words of animals that weren't familiar and took the list home with me that night.

Webster's Dictionary became my new best friend. By looking up the English words I had written in my notebook, comparing them to the Latin roots, and studying the accompanying pictures in the dictionary, I laboriously continued teaching myself to read, write, and speak English. This was in addition to what I was learning in my ESL classes. It was slow going and mentally taxing. Sometimes I gave myself headaches trying to figure it all out, but I made progress. I bought books at the Salvation Army store for twenty-five cents and read aloud as much as I could, not even understanding what I was reading. It was important that my eyes got comfortable with foreign letters. I set a schedule and disciplined myself to study every day. For the first time ever in my entire life, I had no school, no job, no permanent place of my own, no friends, and no money.

I had found a coffeehouse down the street at the corner of Fillmore and Jackson that attracted an international set. It became my favorite hangout. At first, I just eavesdropped on conversations and noted, with growing delight, that I could understand snippets of conversations. Thanks to my zoological Rosetta Stone, I was learning English.

Then I noticed a table of young people, laughing and talking in a variety of languages. I had found my peers. What fun it was to meet energetic exchange students from around the world and make friends with people my own age! Our ragtag group came from Italy, Sweden, Guatemala, Switzerland, Germany, and Russia. *Aha! They're all like me*, I noticed, *speaking English with an accent*. We were so grateful to have found each other—we were all "strangers in a strange land." We became a community unto ourselves.

I remembered that back home in Russia, my eighth-grade teacher used to call my father at the hospital where he worked to say, "Your daughter is really good with languages. And she is only fifteen years old. You should encourage her to study German. She could work as an interpreter."

That probably would have been a great idea if I had gone to Germany, but few people I met in San Francisco spoke German. Speaking Spanish would have been more helpful. I was grateful for the teacher in Russia who had encouraged me to study a foreign language. When someone asked me a question, I would automatically answer in German. That's how I met Karl from Germany, who owned an upscale hair salon.

I spent my days with my melting-pot group of friends at Spinelli's coffee shop on Fillmore and Jackson Street, studying English at the zoo, and discovering how wonderful San Francisco is. The nights, however, were awful when I had too much time on my hands. Inevitably, my thoughts turned to Russia and the family I had left behind. My school. My friends. Was my decision to leave so hastily wise? Rash? Was my time here supposed to be a temporary adventure? Was I meant to stay? I lay in bed at night, going back and forth, asking myself, *Should I stay? Should I go home?* I often woke up with a wet pillow, evidence of my tears of homesickness. My open-date return ticket would expire three months later. The night before it expired, I didn't sleep all night, thinking, *The flight leaves at 9 a.m. This is my last chance to go home.* Making decisions is always difficult, but making a decision that will affect your life once and forever is nearly impossible.

Just when I was seriously considering returning home, serendipity (or what I now call *serendestiny*) showed up again in my life.

On the morning when my Aeroflot ticket expired, I went to look for a job. I took a bus on California Street and ended up in a nice neighborhood, where I saw a woman pushing a stroller. She looked worried. I decided to follow her. A block later, she entered a building and posted a note on the board: *Nanny wanted.*

I could read her note. Perfect! "Nanny" sounded similar to *nannya* in Russian. I understood that she needed help. But when I turned around, she was already gone. I ran outside and approached her.

"Hello, hello, hello!" I tried very hard to speak good English. "I am looking for a job and I can work for you."

I got the job! The woman, whose name was Marian, worked in the film industry, and her husband was a freelance photographer for *Time* and other well-known magazines. They told me that their son was an easy child. "He sleeps well, eats well, and loves to play," they said. They showed me around the house and offered me hundreds of CDs to listen to and magazines to read if I were bored.

From left, top row: my grandfather, Alexander Ivanovich Kim;
my grandmother, White Pearl; a family friend.
From left, bottom row: My father, Alexander Alexandrovich Kim;
his younger sister, Zoya Alexandrovna Kim;
his older sister, Ludmila Alexandrovna Kim (May 3, 1953).

My grandparents' house in Chechnya (1953).
White Pearl's youngest son, Arkadiy, was born here in January 1956.

From left, top row: Victor, my father's cousin; and my father, Alexander.
From left, bottom row: White Pearl holding her youngest son, Arkadiy;
Zoya; my grandfather, Alexander (Chechnya, 1957).

My aunt Zoya (Zoë) and a statue of Vladimir Lenin.

White Pearl (second from the right) and Alexander
(third from the right) with their friends, neighbors, and colleagues
celebrating International Workers' Day (May 1, 1957).

White Pearl, kindergarten teacher.

My parents, Alexander and Klara (1967).

My mother (first from the left) in Red Square, Moscow,
in 1963. Lenin's tomb is behind the group.

From left, top row: Aunt Zoya; Arkadiy; my mother. From left, bottom row: White Pearl; me (on her lap); my grandfather (1973).

My Aunt Ludmila, with her daughter Irina, on the first day of school (1971).

My grandmother, laughing, at a friend's party.

Young Dmitriy with his mother, Galina, and his father, Vladimir (1977).

Dmitriy's grandmother, Sofia, second from the right, bottom row,
and the women's platoon World War II (1943).

Djuna and Livia (1996).

White Pearl's mother, Elena Hvan.

Here I am in America! (April, 1994)

КАЗАКСТАН РЕСПУБЛИКАСЫНЫҢ
ПРОКУРАТУРАСЫ
КЫЗЫЛОРДА ОБЛЫСТЫҚ
ПРОКУРАТУРАСЫ
167901. "Қызылорда қаласы, Черяков көшесі, 1.
7-72-50, 7-61-65.

КОПИЯ

ПРОКУРАТУРА
КАЗАХСКОЙ
ПРОКУРАТУРА
КЫЗЫЛОРДИНСКОЙ ОБЛАСТИ
167901 Кзылорда, ул. Чернова, 1.
Тел: 7-72-50, 7-61-65.

от _21.11.96_   № _13/899-96_

на № ____

С П Р А В К А
о реабилитации

        На основании Закона Республики Казахстан"О реа-
билитации жертв массовых политических репрессий"от
14 апреля 1993 года подтверждается,что _____
___ _Пак Камилле_
19_26_года рождения совместно с родителями,выселенны-
ми _в_ Казахстан по _националь мотивам_ в 19_37_го-
ду,проживал(а) на спецпоселении в _Кзыл Орди-_
енти области с 19_37_года по 19_56_год и он
(она) признан (а) пострадавшим (шей) от политических
репрессий.

Старший помощник
прокурора области
советник юстиции   Пак Ю.И.

КЕЛЕСІ ...
СМ НА ОБОРОТЕ

Above is the certificate of rehabilitation which my maternal
grandmother, Natalia Pak, received on November 21, 1996. It
stated that the Republic of Kazakhstan ratified the act "The Law
of the Kazakhstan Concerning the Rehabilitation of Repressed
Nationalities" on April 14, 1993. Natalia Pak, who was born in
1926 and together with her parents was forcefully deported to
Kazakhstan, was recognized as a victim of political repressions
from 1937 to 1956 from Far East of Russia.

Note: The date on the document is 21/11/96. In Russia the
date goes first, the number of the month second, the year last.

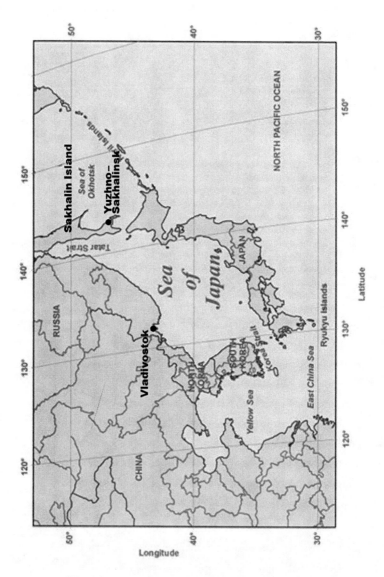

My great-grandparents arrived in Yuzhno-Sakhalinsk,
Sakhalin Island in 1900.

CHAPTER 8
THE ULTIMATE GOOD SAMARITANS

"You must give some time to your
fellow men. Even if it's a little thing,
do something for others, something for
which you get no pay but the privilege
of doing it."

—Albert Schweitzer

❧

One day a woman named Julie was getting her
hair cut at her favorite salon in San Francisco. While
checking her new do, she noticed a note on the mirror:
*A young Russian woman can read in Russian, Latin, and
German. Read works of Russian authors: Pushkin, Chekhov, and
Gogol. Needs a room.* It happened that Julie was a big fan
of Chekhov, Gogol, and Dostoevsky.

When she asked Karl, her stylist, about this, he explained that a friend of his, an émigré from Russia—me!—was looking for a place to stay. "The poor girl is in a critical situation," he told her. "She needs a room. She has no one here. She is a good girl." Karl was working on a documentary film on the Russian poet Mikhail Lermontov, and I was helping with the translations. I had been introduced to him by one of my new American friends.

"I will help you get a job," Karl had told me, and he kept his promise. I received a telephone call from Julie the same day. "I'll meet you at my house on Webster Street," she said. "The cross street is Bush. It's near Japantown." I understood everything she said. "Webster" sounded exactly like the name of my dictionary. "Bush" sounded like the name of the president (George H. W. Bush). Japantown, I knew, was a few blocks from the Korean Center. I decided to walk all the way there. I found it!

I walked up the stairs and rang the bell. "Coming!" I heard Julie calling. When she opened the door, I saw a young woman with a short haircut who was dressed in beige shorts and a white cotton top. Her chocolate-colored leather belt matched her sandals. She was in her early thirties, in great shape, and wearing no makeup. I had already noticed that American women don't wear blue eye shadow and red lipstick like many women back home in Russia do. They prefer a more natural look.

The house had high ceilings and a big kitchen with white cabinets. A turquoise leather couch and a cherry wood oval dining table with a black marble top were also in the kitchen, and everything was simple, spotless, and functional. Julie also had a nice garden with ceramic pots of white orchids in full bloom, a fig tree, and big camellia tree.

Her daughter, Djuna (named after the poet Djuna Barnes), who was a year and a half old, was sitting at the kitchen table. She was wearing a beautiful dress with a flower pattern, a matching cap, and pink sandals. She looked like a doll. Her nanny had just given her a cracker and left for the day. Julie asked me about my parents and how I had arrived in New York City, then she told me about herself. I learned that Julie's mother, Judy, was an artist, and her father, Jack, was a physician. "I grew up in Connecticut and went to graduate school in New York," she said. "I am a writer. I love New York. I also love Chekhov and Gogol. I read their work on my own when I was a grad student at Columbia University."

"I love them, too," I said.

"I write short stories," she continued, "and lately some children's stories as well. Let me call my husband, David, to meet you. You can stay with us. You can have your own room. It's on the second floor and it has a fireplace and a bathroom."

David appeared a few minutes later from his office around the corner. Though he only knew a few Russian words like *horosho* (good) and *spasibo* (thank you), he spoke French fluently and had lived in Italy. Julie and David were incredibly nice people. I moved in the next day. (Of course, I still helped my friend Karl translate as much as he needed. He was a fun person to be around.)

The next night, in their house, I got my first good night's sleep. I had the most comfortable pillows with goose down feathers, a luxurious comforter, and satin sheets. I loved having my own bathtub. All I had was my backpack and a large shopping bag with my first Christmas gifts from strangers: a mug with a picture of Santa, filled with Hershey's Kisses; an oval purple velvet pincushion; Christmas lights; and a photo album. Julie gave me some of her beautiful clothes to wear, shampoo and conditioner for my hair, and bath gel. In Russia, we normally take a shower or go to the sauna once a week, but I soon noticed that

Julie showered twice a day. I started to shower once a day.

"Svetlana," Julie said, "the washer and dryer are on your floor. Please help yourself." But I didn't know how to use them, nor did I know how to turn the oven on and off, or use the microwave. We didn't have microwave ovens in Russia back then. I had a lot to learn. Teresa, a nice woman from Guatemala, came that first morning to clean the house. Julie went to the gym. David was out of town on a business trip. Teresa gave me a tour of the house and did my laundry.

My new little friend, Djuna, knocked on my door at eight o'clock in the morning to wake me up. I got the nickname "Russian Bear" for sleeping late that day. She began learning Russian words and sometimes asked me to say something in Russian. Teresa was also teaching Djuna some Spanish. Djuna could not pronounce "Teresa," so she called her "Teta." We still call Teresa "Teta." Djuna soon grabbed a broom to sweep the floor. She loved being around people who worked in the house or garden. She always asked me to sit next to her in the car or at the dining table and share her favorite animal crackers.

With the compassionate generosity that I soon discovered was their trademark, Julie and David became my extended family and took me under their wings. They introduced me to their fascinating world of intellectual discussions.

David, Julie, Djuna, and I went to New York City in early December 1992. This was my first time back there after having arrived a year earlier. I was very excited to visit New York City as a tourist this time. Djuna and I shared a room at the Westbury Hotel on Madison Avenue and Sixty-ninth Street. I woke up the next morning when I heard her saying, "Room service, room service, room service." She was touching the phone.

"Are you hungry?" I asked her.

"Room service," she said.

"Are you sure?"

"Room service."

"Well, let's call room service."

I ordered scrambled eggs for her and a bowl of oatmeal for myself.

In the afternoons after Djuna's nap, Julie, Djuna, and I went to the Metropolitan Museum of Art, the Whitney, and the Guggenheim. We strolled through Central Park and shopped on Madison Avenue. Julie bought me an Amtrak ticket to go to Philadelphia to visit my friend Natasha and her family, who had recently arrived from Leningrad.

I was in Philadelphia for one day and came back the next evening. We stayed in New York for three more days, then went back home to San Francisco.

In 1993, Julie and David took me back to the East Coast to visit colleges. "We'll pay for you to go to college," they said. Though I couldn't enroll officially because I didn't have my green card yet, I was taking noncredit classes at City College in San Francisco. Julie and David paid for my applications to ten colleges, including Vassar, Yale, Smith, Barnard, UC Berkeley, and Amherst. I had an interview at Vassar. The gentleman who interviewed me had an aristocratic look. He was very serious. "How can you afford to pay for college?" he asked me. I didn't have a good answer for him. *I wish I knew,* I thought. Julie and David wanted to pay for my college, but I could not accept that. It was too much money! "You don't even have a green card," the man said. "We can't offer any kind of loans to you at this point." After this interview, I continued to study English even harder.

No worries. Julie bought me books. Lots of books. Books on every topic imaginable. I threw myself into my studies with great zeal. Even though I was 7,500 miles from home, I was back in my element again. Fortunately, books are more affordable in America than they are in Russia, and Julie, David, and I were all avid readers. Every night around the dinner table, we discussed the events of the day—headlines, politics, what was happening in the world in general, what we would do if we were in charge. We were also reading the classics. These evening conversations were my best and truest education.

You might think it couldn't get any better for me, but it did. Djuna added more joy to my life. She was tiny, with long, golden, curly hair, and she loved to hear the children's stories her mother wrote and read to her. I also read books to Djuna to practice my English. Djuna was practicing Russian. Her first favorite word was *babushka.* Back in San Francisco after our wonderful trip to New York City, she and I loved to go to reading hours at the children's bookstore on Union Street. We usually caught a bus down to the Marina District, which had a view of the Golden Gate Bridge. After our reading class, we met my friends at the café on the corner of Webster and Union streets. We could sit on bags filled with coffee beans and look at an old coffee machine on display there.

Djuna got a kick out of riding on the bus. Her favorite thing was to pull the bell. We could barely walk on the streets because everyone, including young men, would stop to say, "What a beautiful child!"

Among Djuna's favorite books were *Babushka's Doll*, *Doctor De Soto*, *Amos and Boris*, *The Amazing Bone*, *The Five Chinese Brothers*, *Curious George*, and *Madeline and the Bad Hat*. Every time I read the word *babushka*, Djuna put something on her head. "Djuna, you're smart," I told her. "*Babushka* means wearing a handkerchief on your head." She immediately found a picture of a *babushka* in the book and pointed to me. It is amazing how children learn to communicate. Djuna would ask me to read a story to her over and over again. She was the best listener. And if I would pause for a second, she would finish the entire sentence. I would read, "This is…," and Djuna would finish, "George." I would continue, "He lived…," and Djuna would say, "in Africa." I would read, "He was a good little monkey and…," she would finish the sentence, "always very curious." I had so much admiration for her talent for having a feel for the words. After a few weeks, she could recite the entire book. Djuna and I enjoyed reading together.

Djuna's little sister, Livia, was born on December 5, 1994. She was a smiling baby with red hair and a chubby belly. We called her "Buddha."

By then I was living on my own in a one-bedroom apartment on California Street, three blocks from their house. Julie, Djuna, and David invited me over for dinner quite often. I had looked at ads in the *San Francisco Chronicle* to find an apartment in the same neighborhood where they lived. It was not easy to rent my first apartment because I didn't have any credit history. I remember when I received my first credit card. I had to deposit money before I could use it. I realized that it was good thing not to have a credit card until I had a stable job.

I was lucky to have a nice landlord, Peter, who said to me, "I can give you a $50 discount and you can move in immediately." His parents had immigrated to America from China in the late 1950s and he understood me well.

When I was at work, Julie used my apartment as her writing studio to help me out with the high rent. She brought a leather chair, bookshelves, and a nice desk. I lived on the top floor of a three-story Victorian building that had slanted ceilings in the bedroom and living room. It was quite cozy. But I could not sleep the first night by myself. I missed little Djuna knocking on my door or asking me to read to her or take her out to buy a burrito at the corner of Fillmore and California. I missed the family.

"Lini," Livia would ask, "do you speak Korean?" My second nickname was "Lini-Greenbini" (I love green beans).

Djuna always corrected her immediately. "Livia, how many times have I told you that Lini speaks Russian, not Korean?"

"Lini," Livia said to me, "you look like Margaret Cho. I love her. My parents like to watch her shows, too. She is so funny. Did you know that she lives here and her parents owned a bookstore?"

"I didn't know that, Livia," I replied.

"Let's go and watch her show upstairs," Livia suggested.

"Livia," Djuna said, "Lini is not Korean and may not like Margaret Cho. Did you ask her if she wants to watch a DVD? Lini reads books and does not watch TV. Isn't that right, Lini?"

"We can watch the show if it is what the two of you prefer."

"Well, we can watch for a half an hour," Djuna told Livia.

One of Julie's best friends, Elaine, visited us every day. Elaine was taking a creative writing class taught by Tobias Wolff. I was knitting sweaters for Djuna and Julie, and Elaine created a label for my sweaters. "*Sweaters* by Svetlana." Both Julie and Elaine suggested that I start my own knitting business, like Margaret O'Leary, a native of Ireland, who came to San Francisco in 1988 and began designing and knitting sweaters from her city apartment. But knitting sweaters was only my hobby. I had learned to knit from my mother, Klara, when I was eleven years old. Knitting was also a school curriculum. Girls learned to bake and knit, and boys learned to drive trucks, and work with wood.

Julie taught me how to make minestrone soup and grilled chicken with lemon and rosemary. That's how I was introduced to healthy living and organic food. *Simple Living* by Martha Stewart was our blueprint to healthy lives.

I always kept in touch with my parents, White Pearl, my friends, and my neighbors back home. "I pray every day for the family who took you into their home," White Pearl often told me.

I graduated from high school in 1985, the year of *perestroika* (restructuring) and *glasnost* (openness). I remember the day when Leonid Brezhnev, General Secretary of the Communist Party, died in November 1982. He had served longer than anyone except Joseph Stalin. I was fourteen years old. All of my classes were canceled until the day of his funeral. However, I still attended school. The principal of our school brought a table and put a big black-and-white portrait of Brezhnev in the foyer. We were not allowed to speak loudly.

Finally, in the years of *glasnost*, Russians were permitted to read the works of the dissident Russian writers like Vladimir Nabokov, Osip Mandelstam, and Nikolay Gumilev, though I didn't get to read them all before I left. Their works had been published after two decades of Soviet censorship. When I was living in San Francisco, my American friends were surprised that I had not read *Lolita* by Vladimir Nabokov or *Doctor Zhivago* by Boris Pasternak when I lived in Russia.

Although world literature was one aspect of my education in Russia, I read *The Arabian Nights* and works by Emily Dickinson, Edgar Allan Poe, Mark Twain (very popular in Russia), James Fenimore Cooper, Jack London, Stendhal, Theodore Dreiser, Kahlil Gibran, and Jonathan Swift, to name just a few. Reading has always been a big part of Russian culture. Many families have a home library.

I remember the morning of October 12, 1986. I was just about to fix my usual breakfast, one small *butterbrod* (sandwich) with a slice of country cheese and cup of coffee with two teaspoons of sugar, when the phone rang. It was my father calling me. "Grandfather just died in the hospital," he said. "We arrived yesterday afternoon."

"I don't believe it." I burst into tears. "This is not true. I received a letter from him yesterday! He didn't say that he was sick."

"He asked Zoë and Arkadiy to call us to see him. He asked for semolina *kasha* [cereal], and then he fell asleep and didn't wake up. His funeral is tomorrow at noon."

"Irina and I will be there."

I could not believe that my grandfather had died, I guess because I was not prepared, but you can never be prepared for a death of a loved one. Except for that terrifying train accident on his way to Chechnya thirty-three years earlier, he had never had so much as a cold.

Irina and I went directly to the airport and flew to our grandfather's funeral. Our flight was on time and we arrived in Almaty as planned. My grandparents' new house was the third house from the corner. It had a nice-sized garden. All the windows and mirrors were covered with white fabric and his coffin was set up in his bedroom, the second room from the entrance. The coffin was made out of wood and covered with red satin. All of his medals were lined up on a small red pillow to be buried with him. The smell of the dead body filled the entire room. I was scared to get close to my grandfather's coffin, even though it was not my first time to attend a funeral.

White Pearl hugged us. "Oiguuu...Grandpa died." She opened the door. Her eyes were red from weeping, though she was not crying when we arrived. "His spirit left his body. I washed his body and tied it with hemp rope at seven different places. Seven times because of the seven stars of the constellation of the Great Bear, which Koreans consider lucky. Dressed him in a new suit that Zoya bought last year."

A small Korean-style table stood across the room. It was the same shape as a modern coffee table but was about seven inches lower. Traditionally, people sat on the floor or a pillow. *Babushka* served a small bowl of cooked rice, three pieces of fried catfish (my grandfather didn't like fish bones), three thin slices of cooked beef, three hard-boiled eggs, three red-skinned apples (my grandfather loved red-skinned apples), grapes, a bottle of Stolichnaya, and candy and cookies. "Odd number only," said Grandmother. "You want to feed him well before he goes to heaven," she said. "It's important to follow the traditional ceremony.

Otherwise, his spirit will be coming back to our house and will be wandering around. It's not good."

"Grandma, I like to attend weddings, but not funerals," I had told her when I was little. But today was my grandfather's funeral. I worshiped him. I loved him. I already missed him.

His face was a yellow color, but he looked calm. If you had not known him, you could not tell that he was a kind, loving man with integrity. "There was something about his eyes," White Pearl said. "They were different. The light went out of them when he was dying. I knew the spirit had already left his body. He asked my blessings to go to heaven. I didn't keep him long. I knew he was ready for his next journey home, to heaven. I told him that I will see him there."

My grandfather was always grateful for my grandmother, his children, his grandchildren, and his friends. Many people who came to the funeral were sleeping on the floor in the living room. I saw them for the first time in my life. They had come from far away to say good-bye to my grandfather and pay their last respect to him.

It was time to ask for forgiveness, say last words, say a prayer, and spend time in total silence. Only close relatives were sitting around the coffin now: White

Pearl, all her children, her grandchildren.

"He asked if he could go," said my grandmother. "His only wish was to die in his sleep. He was waiting for your father to arrive. Sasha came in the morning to the hospital, and your grandfather fell asleep that afternoon."

"He had liver cancer," said my father. "His skin turned yellow while he was still alive."

I looked down at him. His face looked like it was carved out of yellow marble.

The apples and grapes on the table were from his garden. I was wondering about the bowl of rice on the table. White Pearl could read my mind.

"Please take this bowl and throw the rice outside," she said.

"What is it for, Grandma?"

"I'll explain it to you tomorrow morning. Go and rest."

I did as she said. The first thing I did when I woke up the next morning was to go outside to sweep up where I had thrown the rice the previous night.

I ran back inside. "Grandma, there is not a single grain of rice left."

"That's great news! It means Grandfather left

happy. If you don't see any grains of rice left, that means his spirit exited through the window."

I can't explain what happened. No one had swept the ground outside.

At 11 a.m. the next day, an open-bed truck was waiting outside our house. White Pearl, my parents, Aunt Luda and her husband, Zoë and her husband, my uncle Arkadiy, my cousin Irina, and I were sitting near my grandfather's coffin. The top of the coffin was open. A band playing music followed the truck, which was moving at about two miles per hour. People walked behind the truck to the cemetery, which was five miles away from the house.

When we arrived at the graveside, four men, including my father and uncles, slowly lowered the coffin into the grave. As the lid was placed on my grandfather's coffin and nailed down, White Pearl wailed, "I goo...I goo..." According to the old tradition, women were supposed to wail out loud to let the village know that their loved one had died. My grandmother burned Grandfather's clothes. "I asked his soul to depart from our house." I knew that my grandmother had a deep faith. But to recover from the sorrow of death of her best friend, soul mate, husband, and father of her children, would take not only faith, but time.

Here is my favorite line from the movie *The Crow*: "I believe that imagination is stronger than knowledge, that myth is more potent that history. I believe that dreams are more powerful than facts—that hope always triumphs over experience—that laughter is the only cure for grief. And I believe that love is stronger than death."

Later that year, my parents, Zoë's husband Boris, Aunty Luda, and I went to visit our grandfather's grave.

"I saw the cutest little turtle crossing the road on the way back," I told White Pearl. "I've never seen a turtle near the cemetery."

"It was his spirit. His spirit is happy."

CHAPTER 9
TAKING STOCK

"What is important is to keep learning,
to enjoy challenge, and to tolerate
ambiguity. In the end there are no
certain answers."

—Martina Horner, President of Radcliffe College

Djuna and Livia's father, David, was a managing director in the investment banking division of PaineWebber Incorporated until 1992. He had started to work on Wall Street after he graduated from Harvard University. Julie and David met each other in New York, got married in June 1988, in Farmington, Connecticut, and in 1992 moved to San Francisco, where David became a co-founder of an aerospace and defense component manufacturer. Like all successful business people, David was a workaholic. However, whenever he was on the road, he called every night to say good night to Djuna and Livia. He always tried to be at home during weekends, and he spent his free time going to yoga classes with Julie and hanging out with his two daughters at the coffee shop on Fillmore early in the morning before the whole neighborhood woke up. The girls loved being with their daddy. He always treated them—and me—to hamburgers at Johnny Rockets on Fillmore Street. Julie would not normally allow them to eat a hamburger, so Johnny Rockets was a secret. We ordered milkshakes and Djuna picked out a sixties song on the jukebox.

"What did you have for lunch, guys?" Julie would ask. Djuna was then six years old.

"Secret!" Djuna said.

"I've got it." Julie looked at David. "Johnny Rockets again." He only laughed.

One day, at lunchtime, Julie had a friend visiting her. Djuna loved to greet people and ran to open the front door. Julie's friend had a can of Diet Coke in her hand. "No Diet Coke is allowed in our house," said little Djuna to the guest. We all laughed. Julie didn't buy soft drinks for her children. When Djuna was three years old, Julie introduced her to yoga. Now she has her private lessons at their home. Livia takes yoga lessons, too, and the two girls read for an hour after dinner, every single day, 365 days a year. That's the rule.

"Lini, did you ever read *War and Peace*?" Livia asked me on my last visit.

"Yes, Livia. I read it in the eighth grade. I was fifteen years old."

"I love it," she said. "I read the entire collection of Jane Austen's novels, too. But my favorite is *War and Peace*."

"You are unbelievable. How can you be so unbelievable, Livia?"

"I don't know. I guess that I'm lucky to have nice parents. And Djuna."

"Yes, you are very lucky," I said to Livia.

"I like you, too, Lini."

"Thank you. Livia, do you remember when you were eight years old and you were looking at one of the fashion magazines and saying 'sexy'? Your mother told me that your favorite new word was 'sexy.'" There was an ad with Sarah Jessica Parker for *Sex and the City*, and she'd written "sexy" under the ad with a fat black marker.

"Really, Lini. I don't remember that. It's funny." Livia smiled at me. "I'm happy to know someone like you who remembers me when I was a little girl."

Julie, David, the two girls, and I loved to drive to Green Gulch Farm in Marin County, just across the Golden Gate Bridge, to pick organically grown greens. We also went to the San Francisco Zen Center to bring food to the monks, and we visited the famous Ferry Plaza Marketplace to pick up a fresh loaf of walnut bread, local figs, and cheese from Napa Valley. All of us went hiking in the woods in the morning. In the afternoons, Julie enjoyed a cup of tea called Kukicha, a green tea with one of the lowest amounts of caffeine. Djuna loved to taste the tea, and kept saying, "More, more, more." When Livia turned eleven years old, she started helping a vendor at the farmers market on Sundays from early in the morning until about two o'clock in the afternoon. Djuna also volunteered at her school's library when she had free time. She wants to be a teacher. Livia makes straight A's and excels in mathematics. She wants to be an attorney, but she told me, "It may change, Lini. I still have time."

I had always been intrigued by the stacks of newspapers at Starbucks and the long, cryptic columns of names and numbers in *The Wall Street Journal* and

Investors Business Daily. I began to study these foreign financial codes as if they meant something. Eventually I noticed the legends on the bottom. I got it. The codes were the price of the stock for that day, a percentage of the change from yesterday, and a positive or negative change in dollars or cents or even in a fraction of a cent. I had an *Aha!* moment. Then I practiced tracking a few stocks for myself. I found a lot of abbreviations like P/E (price/earnings ratio) and S&P 500 (Standard & Poor's 500 Index), so I went to the Brown Bag bookstore and bought the *Dictionary of Financial Terms*. (Today, you can just go online and use Wikipedia.) I picked out thirty stocks for my nonexistent portfolio.

After a while I became a millionaire on paper! The disparity between the rich and poor was not only obvious to me, but I was experiencing it myself. I kept hearing about Warren Buffett. Who was he? How did he become the richest man in the world? Why are some people wealthy and some poor? I came from a Communist system where the people had neither power nor money. Only Communist Party leaders and their families had power. Salaries for doctors, teachers, bus drivers, librarians, and engineers were almost all the same, we all dressed the same, and we all had the same apartments and standard furniture that reminded me of office furniture. Soviet people lived in government apartments that were small and crumbling. If you had one child, you would qualify for a one-bedroom apartment, which in Russia was called a "two-bedroom"—one bedroom for your child and one living room where you could sleep. Most of the people in big cities didn't have their own apartment; they had a room in a communal apartment where families shared one kitchen and one restroom.

There were so many things in America that I wanted to learn and experience for myself. Now I immersed myself in the study of mutual funds, bonds, and stocks. I was fascinated by the history of the stock market. I read that in March 1792, twenty-four of New York City's leading merchants had met under a buttonwood tree and signed the Buttonwood Agreement to trade stocks only among themselves, to set trading fees, and not to participate in outside trading activities. With that agreement, these twenty-four merchants founded the New York Stock Exchange. With these studies, I felt as if I'd found my professional destiny.

I hadn't given up my original dream. I remembered (as if it were last week, not last year) blithely telling the man who interviewed me at the U.S. Consulate in Leningrad that I wanted to come to America to become a businesswoman. The challenging, rewarding financial world seemed to be the perfect forum and opportunity for me to make my fortune and my mark. My competitive juices had been stirred. My mind seemed to be a match for the intricacies involved with buying and selling stocks, and the industry had plenty of room for ambitious young people who were eager to throw themselves into their profession.

But there was one snag. When I went for an interview at a small, private boutique investment firm in San Francisco in the financial district, the interviewer told me in no uncertain terms that while my knowledge was impressive, I needed sales experience. One of the principals of the firm asked me, "Why do you want to be a stockbroker? Did you have a stock market in Russia?"

"No," I told him. "We didn't have a stock market in Russia when I left in 1991. Things may have changed. But I think that I will be really good at it."

"At what?" he asked.

"At selling stocks. Many stocks."

"There's no substitute for a face-to-face sales background," he informed me. "Without it, no one will ever hire you. A mind for money will take you only so far. You've got to be able to find clients and keep them."

Initially, I was disappointed, but a few days later I realized that the interviewer had done me a favor by telling me the precise nature of my stumbling block. Now I knew what I needed to do in order to get a job as a stockbroker. I was determined to gain sales experience no matter what and build my "golden Rolodex." The only question was, where and how would I find a sales job?

CHAPTER 10
HAVE YOU EVER SOLD
ANYTHING? WELCOME TO
LANCÔME

"Be a first rate version of yourself, not a
second rate version of someone else."
—Judy Garland to her daughter, Liza Minnelli

❧

My jaunts around San Francisco had frequently
taken me through Union Square. How could they
not? Seven days a week, this tourist mecca teems with
visitors from around the world toting shopping bags
and looking at every store window. The surrounding
streets are lined with jewelry stores with glistening
diamonds in the windows, high-fashion boutiques

with thousand-dollar outfits on the mannequins, and swanky hotels with plush carpets and doormen. But I had my eye on none of those. The week after the interviewer told me that the only thing between me and a stockbroker's license was sales experience, I walked up to the Lancôme counter at Macy's.

The Macy's at Union Square is a city-block long and eight floors high and is a retail wonder to behold. I had been there before, always ready with a "Just looking, thank you." I had been impressed with its classy displays, high-end cosmetics, and cultured sales representatives. My plan was to talk my way into a job.

Now I dressed for the occasion. No, I hadn't shopped at Macy's, Saks, or any of the fancy boutiques in the area. What I had done was take my savings, all one dollar and fifty cents of it, and go to a Salvation Army store on Fillmore Street across from the Kabuki Theatre to purchase an array of cosmetics. That morning, I carefully applied my makeup, put on my best skirt, blouse, and shoes, and styled my hair simply but neatly. The Lancôme counter looked glitzy. The sales representatives wore gray uniforms with nicely tailored long jackets with a gold-tone rose pin (a Lancôme symbol) at the lapels. They looked like models. A perfectly groomed Asian woman was tidying one of the displays as I opened the heavy glass door with the etched Macy's logo in its center. I walked toward her, nodded my head in respect, and said, "I would like to work for you." I had butterflies in my stomach, but determination in my heart.

She looked at me, a little taken aback, and replied, "You're welcome to fill out an application."

Filling out an application, only to never hear back, was not what I had in mind.

"I would do a good job," I told her earnestly. "I would work hard and take good care of your customers. I can sell, too."

She gave me a quick up-and-down assessment. "What experience do you have selling?"

Ah, the old conundrum: You need experience to get a job, but no one will give you a job until you have experience. I knew in my gut that if I told her I was a student with no sales experience, my chance was over. Eager to come up with something to keep the conversation going, I blurted out, "In Russia, I helped my grandmother sell her vegetables and herbs at the market. My grandmother made the best *kimchi* in town."

Her eyebrows went up. I could only imagine that this was *not* the usual response to her question. "Ohh," she said. "I love *kimchi.* You can buy it at the Asian markets in Oakland. Have you been there?"

Seeing that I had captured her interest and that this might be my "in," I continued. "One day, my grandmother was not feeling well and couldn't take her harvest from the garden to the market. She knew her steady customers would miss her and didn't want to disappoint them, so she asked me to take her vegetables to the market and told me to sit next to her friend. I spread out corn, cucumbers, onions, paprika, bay leaves, *purgi* [lettuce], and bunches of cilantro, parsley, and dill tied with black thread. *Babushka's kimchi* was perfectly packed in plastic packs and tied with black thread on the top. Each was just about under one pound, neatly packaged and ready for use. Within fifteen minutes, a buyer stopped by and picked up the ears of corn, examining them for freshness. She asked, 'How much?' and I told her the price. She thought about it, shook her head, and started walking away. I could tell that she had been impressed with the quality of the corn, but the price had been too high. An idea occurred to me.

"I said impulsively, 'You can have everything for half price.' The woman turned back to me, her eyes wide in surprise. She knew this was a good deal. She could go from vendor to vendor, checking their wares, bartering each price, negotiating for each item, or she could get everything she wanted with one purchase. The bazaar was a very busy place. It was interesting to watch people there, selling, buying, arguing, negotiating, and sometimes fighting.

"'It is a hot day,' I told the woman. 'I have the best deal. My grandmother is waiting for me at home. She is not feeling well.' I was convincing my potential buyer.

"'Sold,' she said.

"A half hour later, I was back at my grandmother's house with my empty bucket.

"'What happened?' she asked anxiously. She hadn't expected me back until the end of the day.

"I put a pile of cash in her hand. 'I sold everything for half price.'

"'Aacchh,' she said disapprovingly. 'Why did you do that?'

"'Grandmother, it is simple math. I could sell a little here, a little there, and come home after eight hours with half your inventory sold at full price. Or, I could sell it all in one fell swoop for half price and be home in a couple of hours. We get the same amount of money for a fraction of the effort. It just seemed like the smarter thing to do.'

"My grandmother looked at me. That option had never occurred to her. 'Keep the money,' she said. 'You earned it. If you know how to sell, you can get any job.'"

The Lancôme employee I was telling my story to, whose name was Susan—and who I soon discovered was not just an employee but a corporate vice president visiting the store—seemed impressed with my innovative approach to sales. "You can start next week, part-time," she said. "Thirteen hours a week to start. If you prove yourself, we can increase your hours. We'll call you to start training next week."

They put me in a training class with at least twenty other people. I was in the elevator going to human resources, which was located on the top floor, when I met a Korean guy.

"Hi," I said. "I'm Lana. Are you taking a training class?"

"Hi. I'm Kort. Yes, I am," he said.

"What department are you in?"

"Ladies' shoes. I hear they make good commissions."

"Hmmm…good commissions." *Do my ladies downstairs make good commissions?* I was wondering if I had made the right choice.

I had the best sales training. Our trainer, Denise, had been with Lancôme for ten years. I had one full day of training at the Clift Hotel on Geary Street, where I learned the history of Lancôme, how to build a relationship with my customers, how to apply makeup, how to choose the right skin-care products, and how to offer the best customer service. Lancôme was very popular in Russia and still remains one of the favorite French lines of cosmetics for Russian women.

Soon I was working part-time, but my sales exceeded some of the full-time salespeople's. I was building my clientele book—what I called my "golden Rolodex"—and building relationships with my new and existing clients, which included women from Japan, Russia, Germany, and even New Zealand. A few of my regular clients were male pilots who needed a good moisturizer. We didn't have skincare for men yet, but I convinced them that it was appropriate to use Lancôme moisturizer. "What would people think of me if they saw a women's face cream in my bag?" one of the pilots asked me. "Tell them the truth," I said, "that you want your skin to be flawless."

I sent hundreds of letters, made an endless number of calls, and delivered dozens of shopping bags to women in poor health who couldn't come to the store, didn't walk, or had no car but wanted to look beautiful. Holidays were the busiest times of the year. I remember one Fourth of July promotion in particular, when a client would receive a free gift from Lancôme if a purchase totaled $17.50 or more.

One day I had a customer who had spent over $200 and was asking for ten gifts. I politely replied that we were allowed to give only one gift per person. She still demanded ten gifts.

"Please be grateful for one," I told her. "There are people in the world who don't even have a piece of bread."

After a moment of silence, she said, "I am sorry. I will take only one. I don't think I need that many."

By the end of the year, I had become one of the top salespeople. I received a President's Circle Award and learned that I would be invited on the stage with the chairman of Federated Stores. There were at least a hundred people in the ballroom at the Clift Hotel. This was the first professional achievement of my life. I was grateful for the opportunity. I wore a black velvet dress. My short black hair, red lipstick, and velvet mascara created the perfect look for the evening. Not too much, just right. I was so thrilled to be on stage. I received a Tiffany gold pin with the Lancôme logo, the golden rose.

AnnaMarie, who was my first mentor at Lancôme, and her mother, Immaculata (or, as her grandchildren and I call her, Nini), invited me to see plays and musicals with them and took me on trips to Napa Valley to taste wine. Nini and White Pearl were the same age. I soon felt as if they were best friends because I always talked about one to the other. We have been friends for fourteen years now.

"Lana," Nini said to me, "I am your Italian grandmother."

"I'm proud to have an Italian grandmother."

One day she asked me to model at the charity event she was organizing. We drove down to Millbrae, about twenty minutes from San Francisco, and took a curving road that went down the rolling hills to the Green Hills Country Club. We had a nice California lunch of green salad, grilled lamb, and delicious chocolate cake for dessert. Then it was time to go on the stage to model. I was modeling a dress and a suit. It was so much fun! Both were sold immediately for good prices.

A month before Christmas, AnnaMarie and Nini started planning their Christmas party. They ordered gifts from Gump's catalogs, got a big Christmas tree decorated with ornaments from all the places they had traveled, selected songs by Barry Manilow and Frank Sinatra, made name tags for their guests, and put all the perfectly wrapped gifts under the tree. Invitations to their party were mailed in the first week of December and a follow-up call was made by December 15. Guests arrived for cocktails at 5:30 p.m. and dinner was served at 6:15 p.m. in the downstairs living room. My favorite part was coffee and dessert. AnnaMarie's grandfather had brought a coffee machine from Italy that made even regular Folgers taste divine.

Then, after dessert, Nini announced, "I can hear the bell ringing. It's Santa Claus coming down the chimney. Please go upstairs to the living room on the second level. He has brought wonderful gifts for you all."

There was a Christmas tree touching the ceiling. All the Christmas lights were on. Our Santa Claus was Nini's granddaughter, Milena. "Merry Christmas!" Santa said. "I've brought a bag with gifts for each of you. I have traveled hundreds of miles to celebrate this Christmas with you."

Everyone had to make a wish, open a present, and read the Christmas card that came with his or her gift. Some of them were humorous and we all laughed. It would take three to four hours to open all the gifts before we adjourned.

In 1996, Lancôme promoted me to makeup artist, and I received recognition every year for my work. I also had an opportunity to work with the world's most gorgeous model, Ines Sastre, when she made a personal appearance at the store. I was in a photo with her. She turned to me and said, "I've been traveling to Latin America, home to Europe, and touring San Francisco and New York. My eyes are tired. Are my eyes all red? How do you spell your name?"

"L-A-N-A," I responded. "Despite your hectic travel schedule, you look great." *Even models can have puffy eyes*, I said to myself.

"What a pretty name," she said. "Here is my photo with my autograph for you." She handed me a big photo of herself.

"I will treasure it!"

Ines was sitting in a director's chair. She was wearing a sleeveless sequined dress and high heels. She had just come back from Argentina, and her suntan gave a natural glow to her entire body. Ines is not six feet tall, as you might think, but she has legs that, as my grandmother would say about her sister Gymok, start from her neck.

In the late fall of 1996, I was hired by the Neiman Marcus store in San Francisco as a business manager for Lancôme. They wanted me to build the business at one of the most upscale stores in downtown. I took the opportunity, but I was worried because I would have to be excellent. I had been promoted every year for being one of the highest-producing salespeople. Selling was natural and easy for me. Now I was learning to manage people and teach them how to be top producers. It was something that I had never done before, but I was eager to learn how to manage people by leading them and being a role model. "Lead by example" was my motto. We had so much fun!

I was thrilled to work for Lancôme at the Neiman Marcus store in San Francisco, but I had to get accustomed to a new clientele. They lived in the world of fashion. They breathed fashion. They didn't miss any opportunity to see a new collection. I had many clients from Russia, people who had millions of dollars and called themselves "New Russians." One client was from Vladivostok, where my grandmother grew up. His mouth was full of gold crowns, which were very popular in Russia, and he wore a big gold ring on his right pinky finger. He had a Medusa's head tattooed on his left middle finger. He had come to buy cosmetics for his wife and daughter. We spoke Russian to each other. I hadn't met anyone from Vladivostok since I left Russia.

"I have beluga caviar," this man said to me. "If you want, we can trade for makeup."

"I cannot do that," I replied. "We do not practice that sort of thing at all in America."

"Fine. I can pay. How much?"

"What would you like to drink?" I asked him politely to change the subject.

"Do you offer liquor?"

"No." I was feeling a bit intimidated and trying to stay calm. "I meant tea or coffee, soda or juice."

"Espresso," he said. "And tons of sugar."

I went to get his espresso with tons of sugar from my favorite café on the lower level, just across from the men's designer department. We could offer coffee, tea, and soda for our customers. The store paid for it.

This Russian man purchased almost all of the makeup I had in stock. I sold him as much as I usually sold in a week. Then I called a taxi for him and sent along a few nice gifts for his wife and daughter. That was my biggest sale in all those years working there.

"I love shopping in San Francisco," he said. "Thanks for great service and my cup of coffee. Sorry about the beluga. This is for you as a gift." He started to hand it to me.

"No, thank you," I said. "I don't take gratuities. It is my job."

"Then I'll eat it tonight in my hotel. Great idea. You live by the rules here. And continue to live by your rules."

In December 1999, I was recruited by Prescriptives, which is owned by Estée Lauder, to be the business manager for the largest account at Macy's Union Square. I was interviewing people for the holiday season when something happened I will never forget. A Chinese woman came in for an interview. Her look was simple but neat. She was shy and spoke softly, carefully pronouncing every single word. She held her résumé in one hand and a brown purse in the other. Her name was Kim.

"Please tell me the reason you are applying to work for Prescriptives today," I asked. "Do you have sales experience?"

"No," she said. "But let me tell you something. I need a job. I'm a single mother with two children. I'm from Hong Kong originally. I don't have any sales experience, but you know that Chinese people are good at sales because they are not afraid of any work. I am worried about my children. They are in Canada, where my ex-husband got a job."

"We report goals every day," I told her. "We have so much pressure. Can you handle pressure and long hours? Working weekends and late-night shifts?"

"Please," she said. "I need a job and benefits. Here are some photos of me."

I looked at the photos she handed me. "Wow! Is that really you?"

She nodded. "I am a former opera singer. I'm well known back home in Hong Kong. I will work very hard for you. I'm reliable and trustworthy."

I remembered back when I had walked into Lancôme and desperately needed a job. Susan, the Asian woman, had given me an opportunity. *It takes lots of hard work and discipline to be trained as a performer,* I thought.

"What are you thinking about?" Kim asked me.

"I just remembered something," I said. "When I spoke little English, had no money, and needed a job, someone gave me that opportunity. I remember how exciting it was to get that first check and have great benefits. I'll give you a part-time job. You can start training this week."

Kim became one of my top producers. After the holiday season was over and we had a two-digit increase in our sales revenue, we promoted her into a full-time position. Macy's was located a few blocks from the gateway to Chinatown, a tourist attraction and one of the largest Chinatowns in America after New York City's. Kim worked very hard on building her clientele, particularly among the shoppers from the neighborhood and Chinatown. Her loyal clients and referrals helped her build her business, and she became one of our top producers. She built an incredible business and is now happy and successful. More importantly, she is a good person.

We spoke last week. "I am so grateful to you," she says to me every time we see each other or talk on the phone. I went the extra mile for my clients; so did Kim. We treated every single client like our friend. We had a small award for the top producer every Friday. As a manager, I was focusing on my team, which soon became the highest-producing team in San Francisco and the Greater Bay Area.

One day a friend of mine named Freba invited me to meet her for coffee. I was looking forward to our time together.

"Lana," she said, "I want you to apply for a position as account executive with Laura Mercier. You'll be great. It's a wonderful company."

I had met Freba when I worked at Macy's in 1999. She was a counter manager for the Christian Dior line. Her brother, Matin, was a makeup artist, personally trained by Laura Mercier herself. I faxed my résumé to the VP of Marketing and followed up with a phone call. I was hired and started on Monday, August 21, 2001. My new boss, Carrie, came to San Francisco to meet with me.

"Lana," she said on the phone, "can you pick me up from the San Francisco Airport?"

"Sure. Please send me your flight information."

One of the requirements for my position was to have a car. I had a big territory with eight stores. The company was only five years old and didn't offer a corporate car, so my then-boyfriend (and future husband), Dmitriy, and I went to a Toyota dealership and bought one. It had been a while since I had driven a car. My first, a 1967 Honda Civic, had been donated to a non-profit with a mission to help children with cleft lips.

"Do you want me to take the day off and pick your new boss up at the airport?" Dmitriy asked me Sunday evening.

"No, thank you," I said. "I'll be fine. I just don't like to drive to the airport."

"Do not kill your boss," Dmitriy warned me.

I spent a sleepless night, and then Carrie called me early in the morning to let me know that her flight was slightly delayed and that she would take a taxi. Phew!

CHAPTER 11
To Russia with Love— and a Little Trepidation

"It takes a village to raise a child."
—African proverb

❧

I returned to Russia in April 1996, five years after I'd taken that impetuous trip across an ocean and a continent. I had just received my green card. (People always ask me if it's really green—yes, it is.) I wanted to visit White Pearl, who was not feeling well. I missed my family terribly. I also needed to retrieve my birth certificate, which had been lost in the mail and which was necessary to obtain my U.S. citizenship. When I went to the Russian consulate in San Francisco to get a visa, I was told that I could travel with my Russian passport. I flew to Leningrad with a stopover in Frankfurt. I arrived at Pulkovo International Airport. Nothing seemed to have changed.

"How many pieces of luggage?" the customs officer asked me.

"Two," I answered.

"We need to inspect both suitcases." He pulled one on its side and unzipped it. "Why so many new things with tags?" he asked. "Are you selling them?"

"Oh, no. I brought them as gifts for my big family," I assured him. I didn't want him to think that I was selling things on the black market.

"We need to check your second suitcase," he said next. "You are five pounds over. Each pound is seven dollars for foreigners. You need to pay over there." He pointed to the window across the room.

"I will pay right now. No problem." I had a feeling that something was not right.

"Well, I see a problem." He opened my passport. "Your passport will be expiring soon. You need to obtain a new one." He gave me my passport back.

I went over to pay for the extra five pounds and was asked to wait for my luggage.

Now that I was back in Russia, many conflicting

emotions filled my head. On the one hand, I was looking forward to seeing my family and friends. On the other, I knew that the notorious bureaucratic system could "eat" my papers, and I might never again set foot in America. I had a difficult time trying to make appointments with officials. They told me that one official I needed to see was completely booked, but I saw that his schedule was half-empty.

"How can that be?" I asked the secretary. "I see that you have plenty of appointments available."

She closed the door on me and refused to open it again.

I was shocked. Here I was, trying to spend time with my family, and instead, I was wasting my time trying to book an appointment with a bureaucrat. But I was lucky again. My father had a patient who was supposed to be moved to another hospital that was located near the city where her son, who was a general and had a high position in the government, lived because it was hard for him to travel to visit her. In Russia, we didn't have the luxury of airplanes leaving every hour. We had two or three flights a day to a certain destination.

"I am not moving," the woman told her son. "I found the best doctor. Doctor Kim. He is the head of this department and he sees all the patients, or at least the ones with serious conditions."

The son turned to my father. "Doctor Kim, I guess my mother will stay in the hospital," he said. When he was just about to leave, he asked my father, "What can I do for you?"

"Let your mother stay here."

One of my father's colleagues jumped into the conversation. "Dr. Kim has a daughter who lives in America. She has come home to visit and is stuck with our bureaucrats. It's her third month waiting for her new passport that she will only use once to board the airplane back to America. No one returns her calls. And she was told that it may be a year before she can get another one. The girl is depressed."

"Tell me more," the patient's son said as he looked at him. "What do you mean *stuck?*"

"Well, General," the other doctor said, "I don't know all the details. I know that Dr. Kim would never ask you for anything."

"I need her name and phone number." The general turned back to my father. "Doctor, I'll call you next week. Why didn't you ask me earlier?"

"Well," my father said, "I thought that everything would be fine."

My father gave the general the name of the person who never returned my phone calls, who never would give me an appointment to see him. That was all the information he gave him. I was skeptical that the general would help us. "Papa," I told him when we were alone, "I don't think the general can help me. He didn't even ask me any questions."

My father looked calm. "I do trust him. He seems to be a good man."

"I don't know who to trust here. I have less than a week left before my airline ticket expires. I just feel so bad. It seems that I always cause you and Mom problems." I had tears in my eyes. "We could not even relax."

My friends back in San Francisco were also worried about me. I was terminated from Lancôme for not returning from Russia on time. AnnaMarie, my friend and colleague, came to the neighbor next door who had a key to my apartment and my telephone number. When she called me, I was so happy to hear her voice.

"I received your card from Russia," AnnaMarie said. "Thank you. But you wrote only one sentence, that you can't get out of Russia due to your passport problems. What can we do for you here?" I told her all about my difficulties trying to renew my passport.

"I really don't know what anyone in America can do," I told AnnaMarie on the phone. "My open date to fly back is expiring soon. I haven't paid my rent or my bills for two months, and my car is parked on the street. I've almost lost hope that I will be able to return."

AnnaMarie continued to ask me questions. "When can you come home?"

"I don't know," I whimpered. "Please let our VP at Lancôme know I am so sorry for not being able to return to work on time."

Meanwhile, my mother was looking at pictures that I brought from America. The best gift for my family and friends were photographs of me from America.

"Who is this guy?" she asked me, looking at one.

"My friend."

"Close friend?" my mother curiously asked.

"We're just friends. We see each other occasionally. We are both busy. He always helps me."

"I see. Call him back when you return to San Francisco. He seems to be nice."

"I will call him.

"Do you remember when I told you about my first experience driving a car in San Francisco?" I continued.

"I don't remember the whole story." She was looking for a letter in her cabinet. "You wrote to us that your girlfriend gave you her old car."

"Mom, don't look for it," I said. "My friend Shannon offered me a driving lesson for two hours. Prior to that, I took driving lessons with a driving instructor who was retired and making extra money tutoring people like myself. You remember my bike ride when I was five or six years old? Well, this is similar. Shannon picked me up the next day and we drove to her house, about thirty minutes from San Francisco. I had never driven by myself. I had never driven on a freeway. I had just learned the signs and gotten my first driver's license."

"From the black market?"

"Mom, that's not funny. No, from the DMV. I was driving home after I picked the car up from Shannon's house, taking the Ninth Street exit from the Bay Bridge, and guess what? Everyone was honking at me! I saw the smoke coming out of my 'new' car. The car was a 1967 Honda Civic, and the stick shift did not work well. After a day of driving, I got a blister on my palm. I was born in 1968 [only Russians talk freely about their age!], and my car was a year older than me. Apparently, the radiator needed some water. I pulled over to the side of the road. Who did I call in this emergency? Can you guess?"

"Dmitriy!"

"You are right. But he was in school. Well, a nice man stopped and helped me to get some water and told me to wait until the radiator cooled down. He showed me what to do. After two hours, I started my car and drove home. How did I read the signs on the freeway? I don't know."

"You should definitely call him," my mother said. She was always interested in my friends.

"When?" I asked her. "I am here."

"When you get back to San Francisco." She looked at me, trying to hear agreement in my voice. My mother was so sure that I would be able to go back to California soon.

"Okay," I promised her. "I will if you wish."

A few days later, on the third day after my father's conversation with the general, my father called my mother with great news. "Tell Svetlana that her passport is ready. We can drive together to pick it up."

I was relieved. My father left his work early, and we drove to the general's home.

"Let's get him some gifts," I suggested.

We went to get a bottle of Stolichnaya. When we arrived at the general's home, I stayed in the car because we could not find a parking space. I was already making some plans and a to-do list: (1) Call my landlord and pay the rent. (2) Call my VP at Lancôme and explain about my passport and the bureaucracy. (3) Move my car. (4) Call AnnaMarie and call Dmitriy.

My father came out of the general's home and gave me my new passport. "One lesson you have learned," he said, "is that you never travel abroad when your passport is expiring in three months. Read the instructions inside your passport. You are lucky again. The general is a good man."

My father and I were driving back home (above the speed limit) and talking with each other and not paying attention to the tar on the road. The "road work" sign was not placed properly. Suddenly our car went off the road and flew into the air, then hit the ground and rolled over. The back seat of the car flew out the window. My head was spinning! I was scared to open my eyes. *Is my father alive?*

"Papa!" I shouted.

"Don't scream. I'm here," he said. "Are you *zhiva* [alive]? Give me your hand. Get out of the car."

When I heard my father speak, I opened my eyes. "My God!" He and I were covered with tar from head to toe. We both looked like someone had poured a bucket of tar over our heads. I had a bruise on my right elbow and my head hurt. A car was passing by and the driver stopped. The man, who was towing a car, helped us to get our car out on the road, then he and my father turned our car right side up. The engine worked and the wheels were fine. We were able to drive back home, though slowly. I felt so bad. My father had just taken the car to the body shop, and here we were driving his car with shattered windows, broken seats, and a dented roof. I wished we had sunglasses to protect our eyes. The wind was blowing into our faces.

"I can take you to the hospital right now," Father said. "Is your elbow in pain? How is your head?"

"Dad, I don't have medical insurance," I admitted. "I may be terminated for not returning in the agreed-upon two weeks. Actually, I am fired. " I continued, "Let's focus on the road and pay attention. One lesson for you, Dad, is to pay attention to road signs and not to speed, even if dinner is on the table."

"Thank God we are alive. You'll get another job

and I'll repair the car," he said. "The car is not a problem. I'll take it to the body shop. I know a great guy there who can fix anything."

After a few hours we arrived home.

"What happened to you?" my mother asked. "I had funny feelings. Aunt Luda is here. We were waiting for you for *obed* [lunch], and now it's almost supper time. Auntie made *pelmeni* [dumplings]."

My mother worries all the time. "One day you will be a mother and you will worry the same way about your children."

My father and I went to the hospital to take an x-ray of my chest and right elbow. All the test results came out fine.

My flight was leaving from Moscow the next day, and my ticket was expiring. I spent the night with friends of my aunt and took a taxi early the next morning to the Moscow Sheremetyevo International Airport, which was opened in 1959, with its first international flight to Berlin the following year. I told the taxi driver to take me to the international airport, but instead he drove me to the domestic airport, called Domodedovo.

"Here is the Domodedovo Airport," the taxi driver said to me. "It's $40, including the tip."

"I am going back to the United States," I told the taxi driver.

"Where?" he asked. He seemed surprised.

"I am going to America. I am going to San Francisco," I repeated. "I asked you to take me to Sheremetyevo International Airport."

"You don't look like someone who is going to America," he said. "You have no luggage. You look very young."

"We don't have time to talk. Please take me to the right destination. I will miss the flight."

"Okay, I'll take you there." He shrugged. "No problem."

He was going too fast. "Slow down," I asked him. "I was just in a car accident two days ago."

The driver was silent. I didn't understand why he got mad at me. His mistake in airports was not my fault.

We got there on time. But I was halfway to the gate when I realized that I had left my suit in his car. I ran back. The driver was still waiting for me outside his car, holding my suit. "I knew you would be back. I decided to wait for you."

I gave him a $10 tip.

"That's nice. *Spasibo!* Have a great flight."

"I have to run!"

❧

I boarded the plane.

One of the flight attendants was reading the *San Francisco Chronicle* and talking to himself. "Not this one. This is too expensive. Crazy guy! Who does he think he is…"

He looked at me and said, "I am looking for a used car, Japanese, preferably, the cheapest possible. I want to sell it in Peter." Local people from Leningrad called the city "Peter" from its former name, St. Petersburg.

"No problem," I said. "I can even give you my car for free."

"What?" He was surprised. "Free? How old is your car? What year? How many miles?" He was taking my offer seriously.

"One year older than I am," I said. "1967. One hundred twenty thousand miles." I was losing my patience. And I was starving.

"Hmmm. You need to recycle this car," he grumbled. "It's garbage. Let me bring you some food."

He brought me a sandwich and a bottle of water. Then I took his newspaper and circled all the ads he would find interesting.

When we arrived at San Francisco International Airport, I took a taxi home. I opened the door and fell onto my bed, not even taking my clothes or my shoes off.

A phone call woke me up. It was my friend Dmitriy.

CHAPTER 12
DMITRIY, MY DMITRIY

"To understand the heart and mind of a
person, look not at what he has already
achieved, but at what he aspires to do."
—Kahlil Gibran

꧁꧂

Do you perceive a trend here? My entire life has
been blessed with Good Samaritans, white knights,
heroes, and compassionate people who reach out and
generously help me on my way. My grandmother would
call it karma. Yes, we talk about karma in Russia, too,
although we call it *sudba*—fate or destiny.

Dmitriy definitely counts as a personal hero who
has played an important role in my unfolding saga.
My new American friend, Leslie, introduced me to

him. I first met her at the tennis court in the Alta Plaza Park where I went for my morning walk. She had come to practice tennis but the tennis instructor, Peter, hadn't shown up.

"Peter is not coming," I told the young woman who was waiting for him.

"Where is he?" she asked me.

"I heard that he moved to Florida with his family."

"I used to take tennis lessons from Peter," she continued.

"What's your name?"

"My name is Leslie. And what's your name? You have an interesting accent."

"I'm from Russia. And you?"

"I'm originally from Pasadena, in southern California. I live near Ocean Beach. Ohh...you've got to meet Dmitriy. He's my neighbor. He is the nicest guy."

My friend Leslie loved to play cupid. She was forever trying to fix me up with someone, and I was forever bowing out and begging off. I was too focused on my dream of becoming a stockbroker. I was also working long hours at Lancôme to build up the necessary sales experience. I had no time for a boyfriend.

A few months later, Leslie had a St. Patrick's Day

party and invited me. After I arrived, she impulsively picked up the phone and invited Dmitriy to come to her party, too.

"He's coming," Leslie announced triumphantly, a gleam in her eyes.

I knew she was up to her old tricks, trying to match me up. An hour later, no Dmitriy, so I went to his apartment, just one story below Leslie's, to invite him personally to the party. Galina, Dmitriy's mother, opened the door and welcomed me in. She had a pleasant voice and was very friendly.

"Dima," she called him, "you have a guest."

Dmitriy, a good-looking, dark-haired young man, was in the living room talking with a friend on the phone.

"Hi," I introduced myself. "I'm Lana. Leslie asked me to come down and invite you to the St. Patrick's party." I was speaking very fast.

"Thank Leslie for her kind invitation," he replied. "I'll be there in a few minutes."

I've dodged a date bullet, I told myself as I went back to Leslie's apartment, but twenty minutes later the doorbell rang.

"Lana," Leslie said, "it may be Dmitriy. Can you

open the door, please?"

I opened the door.

"Hello." He handed me a box of chocolates and a bottle of champagne.

Hmmm, I thought, *this one may have potential.* In Russia, people wouldn't think of showing up at someone's house empty-handed. In the hour since Dmitriy had received our invitation, he had cleaned up (and he cleans up well) and had gone out to purchase these gifts. Dmitriy and I became buds. Not only did I get to speak Russian with him, but I also got to practice my English. In addition, he let me drive his Buick.

"Your Russian is perfect." Just one of the dozen compliments he gave me that evening.

"Look. I am from Russia. Russian is my first language." I pulled my red passport out of my pocket and handed it to him.

"I'm surprised. I've never met a Korean person who speaks Russian. I've never met Koreans in my life," he said honestly. "Are you here with your parents?"

"No. I came all by myself in December of last year. Now I live with a nice American family," I explained.

"I admire you for having the courage to come to

America by yourself. I don't think that I could do that." Then he added, "You should come over for my grandmother's *blini*. She makes the best *blini* in town."

Ohh…his grandmother's *blini*. Dmitriy was right. His grandmother did make the best *blini* in the world.

He became my stalwart companion. If I needed to go across the city to deliver some cosmetics to a client, he drove me. Although he was an undergrad student at St. Mary's Catholic College and I was a round-the-clock workaholic, we still found time to go to the movies, to Fisherman's Wharf, and to a Chagall exhibit at the Bowles/Sorokko Gallery, just across from Ghirardelli Square.

During these outings, I gained many insights into Dmitriy's family history. His parents, Galina and Vladimir; his grandmother, Sofia; his mother's younger sister, Tamara, along with her one-year-old son, Maksim; and Dmitriy had all come to San Francisco from Belorussia on February 29, 1992. Sofia's daughter, Ludmila (Lusya, as we called her, or Lucy, as her American friends called her), was already living in San Francisco. She and her husband and two small children, Sasha and Anna, had moved to San Francisco in 1988. They had gone to Italy first and lived in the camp for immigrants for eight months, where they were required to learn basic English and received visas to America.

As a member of the JCCSF (Jewish Community Center of San Francisco), Lusya had arranged to get airline tickets for five adults through the center. Maksim (Max), who was a year old, got a free ride on his mom's lap. JCCSF gave them a loan of $1,500 per person for the airline tickets with no interest for five years. Lusya worked as an RN (Registered Nurse) at Laguna Hospital in San Francisco. Dmitriy called her Mother Teresa. She would give small gifts to her patients who had no relatives living close enough to visit them. They learned more about her patients than the patients' families knew.

Lusya visited her mother, Sofia, every day for at least a half an hour on her way to work. She also dropped whatever she was doing to help her mother or other family members. Lusya was a good mother and set a good example for her two children. Anna and Alex were the reason she moved to America, so that they would have the opportunity to have a better life. Anna is now working as a physiologist in San Francisco. Alex is a medical doctor in Boston. In the spring of 2006, Lusya died from breast cancer far too early, at the age of fifty-six.

The Jewish Community Center in San Francisco offered free counseling to newcomers. Dmitriy still keeps the phone number of a woman named Naomi, a resettlement coordinator at JCCSF, who spoke Russian. The Center also donated two chairs, a kitchen table, and some dishes and utensils to Dmitriy's family.

When JCCSF donated a used car to them—a brown 1982 Buick Skylark—Dmitriy announced, "We have a car. Now we must pass our exams and get jobs."

Dmitriy studied days and nights for his state board examination to get his RN license. The preparation for this comprehensive exam required great mental effort and discipline. Dmitriy was determined to pass the examination and get a job. He passed his test first, then it was his father, Vladimir's, turn. Vladimir was nervous because he didn't speak English well, so Dmitriy was his tutor. Soon Vladimir passed his state board examination, too. And it was then Tamara's turn. Tamara faced challenges because she was taking care of her baby and studying at the same time. But eight months after they arrived, all of them passed the state board exams and got jobs.

Tamara's husband, Nikolay, had come to the States

in 1994. Their son, Max, wants to be a medical doctor to follow in the family tradition. He is a freshman in college in Boston, pursuing his dreams.

Dmitriy's mother, Galina, had taught at the local medical college in Belorussia. At the age of twenty-two, she suffered complications following a bout with the flu. Galina refused to rest because she had an important exam in medical school and she did not want to miss it. She was one of the few patients to have open-heart surgery in Moscow in 1979.

"Doctors at UCSF call her survival a miracle," Dmitriy told me. "All the students come to see my mom every time she has a doctor's appointment. We are lucky to have the best cardiologist at UCSF. When I was twenty-four, I had a crisis—the sickness of my mother and the death of my friend, Yuri. My mother had a severe stroke that paralyzed the right side of her body and took away her ability to talk. I learned that I was responsible not just for myself, but for someone else, too."

Yuri was Dmitriy's friend and mentor. I asked him to tell me about Yuri. I believe that the friends we have are intangible assets in our lives.

Dmitriy began his story, "At the age of twenty-six, Yuri was already a neurosurgeon, then a doctor in the air force. His job was to fly as a second pilot in order to monitor the condition of the pilots during the test flights. It was regarded as the most risky job. His military career ended after he was injured in a plane crash. Yuri received a medal for valor and an honorable discharge from the air force. A few years later, he became a director of a pharmaceutical factory, which was the only one of its kind in the whole Soviet Union. Shortly after that, Yuri was appointed to the World Health Organization, traveling all over Europe, and then a member of the Ministry of Health of Ukraine. Yuri was noticed for all his hard work and promoted to be the first advisor to the secretary of the health department of Ukraine. He had achieved all of this by his late forties. I personally admired him because he was a real down-to-earth person."

Yuri died from a heart attack at the age of fifty-three. Dmitriy was saddened by that tragic news.

"The day of Yuri's funeral," Dmitriy told me, "at our hospital in San Rafael, where we had met and worked together, everyone, including the patients, gathered to mourn him. The administration of the hospital where he worked made arrangements for all the staff to attend the funeral."

I came home from work one day and was surprised

to find curious neighbors. A white rose had been placed on each step from the front of our building, all the way up to the third floor stopping at the door to my apartment. A neighbor downstairs asked, "Who is this lucky woman?"

"I don't know," I answered before going upstairs.

I took my mail and rushed to my apartment. I thought the roses might be for my friend on the second floor, but I opened the door to my apartment and saw Dmitriy holding a big bouquet of pure white roses in full bloom. WOW! Traditionally, white roses symbolize a new love, a tight bond…new beginnings. That evening both Dmitriy and I agreed that we would be moving in together in the near future. I didn't know that it would happen the very next day!

Dmitriy picked me up after work and we drove to my apartment. "I have a surprise for you."

Hmm…I was anxious to know what else awaited me at home after his surprise the day before. Dmitriy asked me to close my eyes before I walked into my apartment. I followed his instructions. "You may now open your eyes, Lana," he whispered in my ear. To my surprise, my apartment was clean and totally empty.

"Don't worry about cleaning your apartment.

I already cleaned everything. Call your landlord now."

"WOW! What a surprise, Dmitriy!"

I will always remember the fall of 1996 (after I returned from my trip to Russia), when Lancôme invited me to assist with the grand opening of Bloomingdale's in Palo Alto. There was only one problem: Palo Alto is forty miles away and at the time I had no car. Dmitriy drove me there every day and did his homework while waiting for me in the parking lot. I knew he had an important test to study for, so I told him that I could take a bus or a train, despite a bad experience I'd once had when I took a bus from San Francisco and the fact that it took three hours to get to Palo Alto.

Dmitriy gave me a surprise present. I had splurged on a pair of Gucci sunglasses as part of my upgraded wardrobe for Lancôme. I was proud to wear something that symbolized my growing professional success and I was upset when I lost them. The next day, a small shopping bag from Neiman Marcus was waiting for me on the passenger seat when I opened the car door for our daily trek to Bloomingdale's. Dmitriy had tracked down the exact pair of Gucci sunglasses and bought another pair for me. He spent half his savings.

Dmitriy makes me feel important. He is what

White Pearl would call a "genuine" man. A man you could spend your life with.

In the fall of 1997, we went to visit Vadim, Dmitriy's childhood friend who had immigrated to Israel from Belorussia, right after Dmitriy left for America. We flew from San Francisco to Tel Aviv. In Israel, security was tight. Dmitriy and I were not used to seeing that many security officers at an airport, and, in addition to that, all of them were carrying weapons.

"Don't worry about it," Vadim said, as though he knew what we were thinking about (I guess it was obvious). "In Israel, we do not pay any attention to it."

Driving on the freeway Vadim offered to show us one of the smallest and oldest towns, Akka. "It's on our way. You will like it."

Akka looked more like a medieval citadel. We walked through the old town, listening to street musicians playing "Michelle," a song by the Beatles. Later that afternoon I saw a street vendor selling blintzes filled with country-style cottage cheese. It tasted like the *blini* that Dmitriy's grandmother made. We bought cheese, grapes, local pita bread, pilaf, falafel, and sesame candies. Dmitriy and I love tasting local and authentic food when we travel.

After a wonderful lunch, we drove to Vadim's home in the town of Nahariya, located on the Mediterranean Sea just south of the Lebanese border.

Vadim told us, "You can't say you were in Israel if you don't visit Jerusalem."

"Would you help book a tour for us?" I asked him.

The next day Dmitriy and I were on a bus trip to Jerusalem.

Jerusalem is breathtaking!

"Don't forget to visit the Wailing Wall in Jerusalem," Dmitriy's grandmother, Sofia, had told us before we left. "It's said that if you write your wish on a small piece of paper and slip it into the cracks of the wall, your wish will come true."

We visited the Wailing Wall. Dmitriy and I wrote down our wishes and slipped the papers into the cracks of the wall.

An then both of us walked into the Church of the Nativity, one of the oldest and most sacred places in the world, built in the center of the city of Bethlehem. We entered (nearly crawling) through a very low door (less than four feet high) called "The Door of

Humility." Our feet touched the original Constantine mosaic floor. It felt like we were walking on centuries of human history. I saw the beauty of five rows of Corinthian columns, the golden mosaics on the walls, numerous lamps, and the sanctuary in the far end of the basilica. Dmitriy and I walked to the sanctuary and found the winding stairs that led us to the Grotto of the Nativity, an underground cave. I felt that something was going to happen and my heart started beating fast when I was walking down to the grotto. I asked Dmitriy to hold my hand. Just as we stepped on the marble floor, we were bathed in a pure light. I felt like sun was shining inside the grotto. There was a fourteen-point silver star set into the marble floor to mark the place where it is said that Jesus was born. Dmitriy held my hand and asked quietly, "Lana, will you marry me?"

"Yes!" Big tears rolled down my cheeks.

Dmitriy opened a little red box and put the ring on my left ring finger (in Russia we wear it on the right hand). Just that morning I had written my wish at the Wailing Wall, and my wish had come true!

To celebrate our engagement we headed to Eilat, with a stop at the Dead Sea. Driving on the road we noticed something that looked like an iceberg in the middle of a desert.

"We're approaching the Dead Sea. You'll see salt on the shore," Vadim explained.

"Why do they call the sea 'dead'?" I asked him.

"It is dead. No fish or plants. The water is too salty. You can't swim in it, only float."

"Really?" I was excited to experience that for myself.

I had so much fun floating in the unusually warm and buoyant mineral-rich water. After a day spent at the Dead Sea, we reached our final destination. Eilat was a great choice.

"It's amazing!" The Red Sea. I looked at the most still surface of any water I'd ever seen in my life. "Look, Dmitriy. No waves!" I held my breath.

We spent most of the day snorkeling in the crystal-clear water, discovering the underwater world and encountering the region's magic. When the sun went down, the Aqaba Mountains across the sea appeared a bright red. I understood then why it is called the "Red Sea." We strolled on the seashore under a starry night with a fresh sea breeze. We lay down on the sand, listening to the waves as they crashed into the shore. That was a night to remember.

When we came back home to San Francisco, everyone was asking us, "When is the wedding?"

"Next year," we kept telling them—for the next six years.

"This year we'll get married," Dmitriy announced.

"We can't postpone our wedding any longer," I said. "Six years is enough."

"Let's go to Las Vegas and get married at the world famous Little White Wedding Chapel," Dmitriy suggested.

"Little White Wedding Chapel? I've never heard of it."

"I thought that you might like it." Dmitriy smiled. "Frank Sinatra, Michael Jordan, and your favorite actor, Bruce Willis, all got married there."

"Well, if Bruce Willis got married there...I'm convinced." I beamed.

"So be it! I'll book a trip." Dmitriy went to check his calendar.

"How wonderful!"

We arrived in Las Vegas.

When our limo pulled into the White Wedding Chapel's Tunnel of Love, the blond female driver opened the door and said, "Here you are." Everything was white—the white Victorian chapel, the white doves, the white roses, the white candles, the white balloons, my wedding dress, and even our limousine.

A camera filmed us as we walked into the chapel, which was beautifully decorated. Traditional wedding music played as we slowly walked down the aisle.

"Dmitriy and Svetlana, this is it. This is your big night," announced the minister.

Dmitriy and I became husband and wife on August 18, 2003, at 10:10 p.m.

Las Vegas was the perfect place to get married. The city hall was open 24/7, and we waited for only ten minutes to get our marriage license.

"Your marriage must have been made in heaven," White Pearl told me when I last visited her. "Just like mine was," she added. "You found your soul mate. I'm happy for you."

CHAPTER 13
UP AGAINST (THE) WALL STREET

"The true worth of a man is to be
measured by the objects he pursues."
—Marcus Aurelius

At seven o'clock in the morning on July 11, 2001,
ten years after I escaped from Leningrad to live in
political asylum in America, I stood in the Nob Hill
Masonic Auditorium at 1111 California Street, near
Taylor Street, along with 1,315 other people, to be
sworn in as a citizen of the United States of America.
I had dressed nicely and looked at myself in the mirror
before I left "for good luck," as my grandmother had

taught me. San Francisco weather in July reminds me of Leningrad. It was nippy, foggy, and had rained for many nights.

The program started with musical selections, the presentation of the colors, and the National Anthem. After taking the oath of allegiance, all new citizens received greetings. *I've waited for this day for ten years,* I thought on the way out. Back then I was thinking that ten years to wait to become a citizen was like a century. A few weeks later, I received a letter from the White House. I opened the envelope and read the letter inside.

Dear Fellow American:

I want to congratulate you on reaching the impressive milestone of becoming a citizen of our great nation...

The United States is a land of unparalleled natural beauty, vast opportunities, and freedom. It is home to people who have been drawn to our shores from all over the world and who share a common love for life and liberty...

Together we must strive to safeguard the freedoms we hold so dear, not only for ourselves but for future generations.

Hillary and I welcome you as a new citizen and extend our best wishes for much happiness in the future.

Sincerely,

Bill Clinton

I felt a responsibility to give back to the people of my new country. I felt grateful that America was now my home. I had been told all along that I couldn't be hired to work in financial services unless I was a U.S. citizen, but now I had my résumé and citizenship. I was ready to knock on the doors of brokerage houses in the financial district. Then I realized that my new passport would not be mailed to me for another month. I went anyway to practice my pitch.

Persistence paid off. The path was now clear for me to pursue a career as a stockbroker. This was the opportunity I'd been waiting for, for ten years.

On January 11, 2002, my birthday, I called Dmitriy and announced, "I just received a letter from a headhunter!" The letter said that PaineWebber was looking for individuals like me with great sales experience. I was invited to attend their open house. Dmitriy and I went to the conference room on the twentieth floor where about thirty people of all ages, mostly men, were assembled.

The PaineWebber representative opened the meeting. "What a great turn-out," he said. "Thank you so much for being with us tonight." He told us about his personal experience at PaineWebber and then he shared what it took to be a successful stockbroker.

"The first year you will work approximately ten to twelve hours a day. You need to be here, at your desk, at 4:30 in the morning. You have to have an established network of people, or find clients quickly. You may ask your parents, friends, and people you know to invest money with you." At that, a few young men excused themselves and left. By the end of the second hour, more people had left.

Dmitriy looked at me.

"I get it," I whispered to him. "I know what you are thinking. I am staying. I want to fill out an application form."

After the meeting was over and to the few people who looked serious, the presenter said, "If you are still interested in scheduling an interview with us, please fill out this form with your contact information and we will call you in a few days."

I filled out the form. It was almost nine o'clock in the evening. Both of us were ready to go home.

"Do you want to pursue this?" Dmitriy said to me in the car.

"Yes, absolutely," I answered.

"Do you want to go to your work in the middle of the night?" he asked me. "You'll have to wake up at two o'clock in the morning. And the parking will cost you $20 a day. Or even more."

"I can take a bus," I replied.

This was my big chance. I knew about PaineWebber, of course, because I had a friend, David, who worked for them. But I was determined not to ride his coattails, so I had not even mentioned on my application that I knew him. PaineWebber was meticulous about who they hired. They conducted an extensive battery of interviews designed to weed out anyone who would not be an excellent prospect for the firm.

My friend AnnaMarie has always been one of my biggest cheerleaders. When I told her about it, she said, "That is marvelous. You will do so well. I am so proud of you."

My first day of the application process with PaineWebber started with an hour-long personality test. My score was above average. Then they focused on customer service and building a clientele. By now I had almost eight years of experience in sales. I was chosen to come back for the next round of interviews, in which we were asked to prepare and present a business plan. Thanks to the Brown Bag bookstore and many years of reading every book on business and on investing that I could get my hands on, I was able to design and deliver an organized and logical business plan of twenty-six pages that would lead to bottom-line profits. My self-study education paid off when the interviewer told me that mine was the best plan she'd seen in years. I was asked to come back for another interview. This one tested my knowledge of basic investing. Once again, my years of late nights of studying charts and graphs and the history of Wall Street reaped the desired results. Finally, a background check, a drug test, and a bankruptcy check were conducted. I passed everything.

I was hired. I found out later that I was the only female selected from the group. There were, in fact, only five females in our office of sixty brokers. I worked and studied twelve hours a day. Dmitriy and I had no days off, but we were happy with our lives. We had goals, and we wanted to reach our goals. Of course, this is not my recommendation for everyone. My typical day would start at 4 a.m., when it was 7:00 a.m. in New York City and the New York Stock Exchange (NYSE) was already open. Every day, I networked until 9 p.m.

But eventually this schedule began to catch up with me. One night, I phoned Dmitriy. "Can you pick me up?" I asked him. "I'm in my office, and I'm so tired I can't even drive my car."

"Lana," he said, "remember, this is a marathon. It's not a sprint. The journey is more important than the destination. I'll be there shortly. Wait for me outside."

I wanted everything fast. I had been waiting for ten years for my dream to come true. We live in a fast society. It was not easy to be patient. The post-9/11 market was sliding down after a decade-long bull market. So I worked even longer hours.

"Dmitriy," I defended myself, "this is a bearish market. Everyone is working very hard in our office. Everyone is selling stocks, but too few people want to buy."

"I know you," he told me. "You'll do well. This is not the first puzzle in your life. You've built teams and managed millions of dollars during the last few years. Remember, our health is our wealth. Who needs all that money if you don't have health and can't enjoy your life?"

I also love the wisdom of my friend, Amy, who gave me a wonderful book, *Thoughts on Wisdom*, one day when we had coffee together. She wrote, "My life—I suppose it has much resembled a blue chip stock: fairly stable, more ups than downs, and gradually trending upward over time."

I read the following in an article, "Stock Market Downturn of 2002," on Wikipedia:

> As of September 24, 2002, the Dow Jones Industrial Average had lost twenty-seven percent of the value it held on January 1, 2001: a total loss of five trillion dollars. The NASDAQ subsequently lost nearly eighty percent and the S&P 500 lost fifty percent to reach the October 2002 lows. The total market value of NYSE (7.2) and NASDAQ (1.8) companies at that time was only $9 trillion, for an overall market loss of $9.3 trillion.

Despite all the losses, however, my good fortune continued. Don, a man raised in Harlem, was one of the finest individuals I've ever known. He became my mentor as well as a good friend. Don received his MBA from the University of San Francisco. He worked as an options trader on the floor of the Pacific Stock Exchange for eighteen years. He also served in the marines in Seoul in the late 1960s. Don introduced me to many things that became staples in my life.

The first time we met, on a Monday morning for a weekly company meeting, he asked if I was Korean.

"Don," I told him, "I'm of Korean descent, but I'm from Russia. I've never been to Korea or any countries in Asia."

"Do you speak Korean?"

"No, I don't. My grandmother's parents moved to Sakhalin, Russia, in 1900, during czarist times."

"That is fascinating," he said. "We'll talk more."

Don came to the office at three o'clock every morning and read books for an hour every day before the stock market opened in New York. He kept dozens of business, spiritual, and history books on his desk. Soon we started to exchange books.

"You will make a great financial advisor," Don told me one morning. "You know what you should do? Start working on your designations. The first one is certified financial planner (CFP). It takes about two years to complete the courses and pass the exam. It covers the fundamentals of financial planning, estate planning, investment, taxation, and retirement planning."

On his advice, I enrolled at Kaplan College. I successfully finished the CFP program in two years, still working seventy hours a week. It felt rewarding to pass my last test. When I received my CFP and my RFC (Registered Financial Consultant designation) in 2004, I thanked Don for his wise advice.

"Congratulations, Lana." He shook my hand. "Next, I think that you should consider applying for a Master's of Science in Financial Services. Keep your mind sharp. Never stop learning. Remember that this is a business of rejections. You need a thick skin. Don't take things personally. It's about trust. Trust is built on a foundation. A foundation is the relationship. Listen, listen, and listen to your customers. Make them feel important. Don't try to impress them with everything you know. Stay humble. You have a great advantage in that you speak Russian. Many Russians are doctors, dentists, and entrepreneurs. This could be your niche market."

In July 2003, I became one of the founders of the Russian-Speaking Professionals Group, a networking group operating out of San Francisco.

Don continued to mentor me. "Never doubt, be confident," he'd say. Every time he spoke, I would write it down. I kept notes on everything he said.

Accounts assigned to me required a lot of attention because many of my new clients were heavily invested in high-tech stocks and had taken a big hit. I treated their businesses as if they were my own. I had the mentality of an entrepreneur.

"Your wallet should be like a clam," Don said to me. "Hard to open. And you want to be like a squirrel. Prepared for a hard winter." I followed this advice, too. "Live below your means," he advised. "Save as much as you can. You must invest, Lana. Inflation will eat your money if you keep it under your mattress. Buy low, sell high. Save money and invest in stocks. One day you will remember my words. Buy stocks for yourself first, so you know how your customer feels when buying his or her stocks. You are familiar with the word 'hyperinflation' because you are from Russia. Russian people can't keep cash because of hyperinflation."

"Yes, indeed," I replied. "I know that term well."

Back in the old days in Russia, people, my parents included, saved for many years to buy a car or to simply have a phone line. We didn't even know about the concept of car dealerships. Everything was arranged through your job, including overseas trips and even entry into sanatoriums. By August 1998, the money my parents had saved for a new car was barely enough to buy a stool. My father told me that his wages were delayed by three months. Coal miners were on strike for unpaid wages. I read an article on the Russian financial crisis. It said that by August 1, 1998, there were $12 billion in unpaid wages owed to Russian workers. Later, I read that the International Monetary Fund and the World Bank had sent financial aid to stabilize the Russian market, but it was revealed that about $5 billion out of the $22.6 billion of the IMF (International Monetary Fund) money had been stolen when it got to Russia.

Last year, I saw a book by Sidney Poitier, *The Measure of a Man: A Spiritual Autobiography*. I thought of Don and bought the book, and sent it to him. I knew he would enjoy reading Poitier's inspiring, true story. Don called me when he received my gift.

"Lana." He sounded great on the phone. "Thank you very much for Sidney Poitier's book. As you know, I grew up in Harlem. Poitier is my idol. He is a man of integrity."

Just like you, I thought.

"How are you doing, my friend?" Don asked me.

"I feel like I'm a psychologist," I said. "My clients often tell more than I want to know about them. We live in America, where people discuss just about anything, yet they will not talk about their personal finances. I have learned that this is because conversations about money pull at so many emotions. Why doesn't anyone teach the positive power of money?"

"You should read a book by Brian Tracey," Don

suggested. "Read *The Psychology of Selling.* Listen to his CD, *The Psychology of Achievement: Develop the Top Achiever's Mindset.*" I wrote these titles down. "Do you know why people fail?" he asked.

"There are many reasons, I think."

"Agreed," he said. "I've learned that people quit too soon, being just a few inches away from success. There is a true story of a man who moved to California during the Gold Rush. He wanted to find gold and be wealthy. But he gave up on digging for gold, sold his equipment, and moved back home. The guy who bought his equipment decided to continue digging in the same hole and found gold."

Due in large part to Don's mentorship, I was honored by being voted into the UBS PaineWebber Advisor Award for Outstanding Achievement. I spent three weeks in New York City for intensive training. The first day, we had to sell stock in front of a camera. A few trainees failed and were sent back home. This meant that this day was their last day of work. Soon it was my turn. I don't know why, but I was scared of the camera. I chose Microsoft stock because I was familiar with the company's history and had heard of others who had pitched MSFT (the stock symbol for Microsoft) and passed the test. This was no time to take risks. I looked at a spot on the wall and paid no attention to what my jury might say to me. I thought they were not happy with my speech, but I learned later that they were fascinated by my Russian accent.

Our group visited the New York Stock Exchange. The next day we had a meeting with CEO Joseph J. Grano, Jr., who introduced himself as simply Joe Grano. Joe was very approachable. He had left college at the age of nineteen and gone to serve our country in the Vietnam War. We learned that he had started as a mail boy at the brokerage firm and worked his way to be one of the top stockbrokers at Merrill Lynch. "Every 'overnight success,'" Don told me, "is preceded by years of struggle." He passed me a piece of paper with another quote: *The rewards of victory far outweigh the pain of the struggle.*

One Friday night, Don and I wrapped up a long week of work. As we headed out the door, he stopped, turned to me, and said, "Lana, you will go far because you are a *good* person. Please give my best regards to Dmitriy. Take it easy this weekend. I'll take you to the Pacific Stock Exchange to meet my colleagues on Monday."

"That would be great! See you on Monday at 4 a.m.!"

I told Don how, when I was still new to America,

I once deposited a check in the trash at Wells Fargo Bank because I didn't know how to use an ATM machine. A roommate I had back then told me I could use the ATM for a deposit by dropping the envelope into a slot. I followed her instructions and dropped my envelope with a check into the only tiny slot I saw. Then I got on a bus on Fillmore Street to go to work. A man ran for one short block after the bus yelling, "She dropped a check into the trash slot!"

I picked up a newspaper on the seat and pretended that I was reading.

"He really likes you," said the bus driver.

"Stop, please!" the man kept yelling. "She dropped her check in the trash slot."

The bus stopped, and bus driver said, "You need to listen to what he is saying." I got off the bus.

I followed the man. He asked the security person to open the trash receptacle. Sure enough, my first check was in there. Then they showed me the right way to deposit a check. After all that, I was late for work and my manager didn't believe my story.

I also told Don about my first trip to an American supermarket, the Safeway on Webster Street near Japantown. When I went there, I remembered my trip to the local bakery in Leningrad with bare shelves, which begins my story. I still could not read English. I decided to buy canned food, as it was popular back home. I didn't know that I was buying pet food.

"Are you going to get a kitty?" a roommate asked me.

"No," I said. "This is for dinner."

"Oops! You bought cat food. Let's go back to Safeway." She grabbed the bag. "I know that pet food does not exist in Russia. I understand where you come from. You poor thing." When we arrived at the grocery store, she approached a customer service clerk and said, "My friend doesn't read English. She accidentally purchased the pet food for dinner. Here is her receipt."

"No problem." He took the receipt. "I'll take the return. Didn't she see the picture of a cat on the can? Never mind." He gave me the cash. Then my roommate walked me through each department and explained everything: Mexican food, Asian food, frozen food, pasta, low-fat food, barbeque sauce, cookies, and fresh produce. It was winter, and we had fresh strawberries, grapes, apples, mangos, and pineapples—fruit I had only seen in books!

"Well, it was a learning experience. Remember that our character is like steel that must be hammered to become hard. As swordsmiths forge steel, we forge our own character," said Don.

Once again, I realized the value of what my grandmother had told me years ago: "Embrace all that life throws at you, good or bad. Neither of them will last forever. Life is a gift from God, and it's up to you how you use it."

Gurumayi describes the essence of life in a beautiful way: "In truth, the gift of life must always be recognized and never be taken for granted. Why is life so precious? In Siddha Yoga philosophy, we recognize that in this human life we have a rare opportunity. We can transform an ordinary perception of this universe into an extraordinary vision. To be on this planet and to behold the universe from the divine perspective is a sign of an illumined heart. To put this vision to best use in the best way possible is a human being's highest duty."

CHAPTER 14
FINDING A FEMALE MENTOR

"The meeting of two personalities
is like the contact of two chemical
substances: if there is any reaction, both
are transformed."

—Carl Jung

I was grateful for my rewarding career as a stockbroker—for the opportunity to fulfill my dreams, and to be able to help others achieve their financial dreams. But by 2006, I was getting itchy feet. I was ready for something new.

I was blessed to have several male mentors, but I yearned to have the opportunity to learn from a female mentor. Unfortunately, these are few and far between in the stockbroker profession. You may have heard that this is a highly competitive industry. What you've heard is true. Women on Wall Street are often so busy trying to climb the ladder of success themselves that they are not interested in or willing to lend a helping hand to someone else on the way up the same ladder. I had studied the businesswomen and the women on the boards of women's organizations and was particularly impressed by a woman named Edie. She had a list of accomplishments as long as my arm, but what really got my attention was her visionary work to help women start and run successful businesses.

My good friend *serendestiny* showed up again. I got a call from my friend Julie, my former colleague, who had worked with me for the Laura Mercier company.

"Lana." Julie was excited. "I will be meeting with my client at the conference in Dallas. I thought of you today because Edie, someone you have said you admire and want to meet, will be speaking at the same conference. Maybe you can meet with Edie. Do you want to come with me?"

"I don't know," I told her. "I'm busy right now."

"This was your dream. I just wanted to let you know." Julie had gotten my interest.

"Hmm. Let me think. I'll call you back."

The event was supposed to draw hundreds of professional women from around the country. It sounded like the perfect place to find my mentor. I decided to go.

As soon as I walked into the Sheraton Hotel in Dallas, I was overwhelmed (in a good way) by the energy of positive, powerful women talking, laughing, sharing, and freely offering assistance and advice. It was nirvana.

At one point in the conference, I spied Edie across the room. Here was my chance. I walked over to her table and stood to one side until she finished the conversation she was having. As soon as she was finished, I extended my hand and said, "I am here because of you. I came to meet you."

Edie smiled at my boldness and hugged me, then got straight to the point. "I'd like to talk to you more, but right now I need to catch a plane back to Washington, D.C." To my surprise, she took out her business card and wrote her cellular phone number on the back. "Call me on Friday," she said as she pressed her card into my hand and headed off to the airport.

As invited, I called her office on Friday. I did not dare to call Edie on her cellular phone yet. I spent a week trying to reach her. Her assistant kept saying, "Edie is on the phone. Do you mind calling back?" I made dozens of calls over the next few weeks, but Edie was always on the phone. One day I decided to call her on her cellular phone. She picked up on the first ring and whispered, "I'm in the Senate. May I call you back? I'm so glad you called. I'll call you this Sunday at 9 p.m., your time."

That's the end of that, I thought. *I'm getting the brush-off.* Imagine my surprise when my phone rang Sunday night and it was Edie. It was midnight in Washington. She wasted no time. "What do you need from me?"

"I want you to be my mentor."

"Okay," she said. "Why should I mentor you? Send me an e-mail with your bio. And I'll get back to you."

I went to my computer and sent her a brief e-mail.

Edie responded immediately: *Who are you?*

I flashed back to my interview with PaineWebber and realized that what I said in the next few sentences would either get my foot in the door or get me kicked out. Edie was smart. What a great question she was asking me. *Who am I?* That is a tough question. I wrote in my e-mail to her, *As a child, I had the wildest dream to live in America!* Then I told her how I escaped from Russia and found my way to work as a stockbroker.

Svetlana, she wrote back, *this is incredible. I am amazed. I want so many people to know you. Call me.*

Edie and I have talked to each other every day since then. In November 2005, Edie invited me to fly to Washington for the Congressional Reception for Senator Debbie Stabenow hosted at Edie's house. It was my first trip to D.C.

The taxi driver drove me across the Potomac River (which looked like the Neva River in Leningrad). The low bridges decorated with statues, the columned buildings, the memorials all reminded me of Leningrad. *This is the city I would love to live in,* I thought immediately.

Two weeks later, Edie invited me to join her in Greece. She was nominated to receive the First Global Athena Award. I felt honored to be invited to the ceremony and to celebrate her achievements. When I arrived in Athens, I went straight to the hotel. Edie and her husband were waiting for me in the lobby to take me to dinner.

Athens seemed to be noisy and crowded at first, but I got used to it. I noticed immediately that the Greek people were friendly. The colossal Acropolis (which means "upper city") and Parthenon, the magnificent temple of the Greek goddess Athena, took my breath away. The Plaka, the oldest section of Athens, located right at the foot of the Acropolis was open for pedestrians only, but you still wanted to watch out for motorcycles, which were the perfect vehicles for the narrow, ancient streets of Athens.

Many people call Edie a "connector." Back in the States, she e-mailed me one day and asked if I was interested in attending the Committee of 200 Annual Conference, which happened to be in San Francisco in the middle of December.

I thanked Edie for her invitation and faxed back my registration form. The meeting was held at the Four Seasons Hotel. On my way there, I bought a bouquet of flowers. When I gave the flowers to Edie, she said, "Thank you very much. I love flowers! Let's share them with all the women here." She asked a woman at the registration desk to put the bouquet in a vase and keep it there.

Edie and her team were busy working on the organization of their annual Diversity and Women's Leadership Summit and Gala, to be held in Washington, D.C. When she offered me a speaking role on the panel, I got so excited that I more or less became a recruiter for the conference for the next month. I spoke during the afternoon of November 17. Don, my mentor at

UBS PaineWebber, and twenty-one other friends came to support me. When the day came, I felt strange. I wasn't nervous, but I had an odd feeling. Right after the panel presentation, I received a telephone call from Dmitriy. "My grandfather Yakov just died."

"Dmitriy, I'm on the way to the airport right now."

I looked for Edie and found her sitting on the steps in the ballroom and writing thank-you notes. When I told her that I had to leave for a funeral, she hugged me and said, "I'm so sorry to hear about Dmitriy's grandfather. You did a great job. I'll call you later."

I took a cab to Edie's house. Her husband, Joe, was home and let me in to get my suitcase, which was already packed. Then I got into the cab waiting downstairs and went to Reagan National Airport. I was lucky to get on a flight and got to San Francisco that evening.

❧

After eight months, Edie told me it was hard to mentor me because I was in San Francisco and she was in Washington. I decided to let Edie know that I could move to Washington, D.C. What else could I do?

"When can you come here?" she asked.

"When do you need me?"

"In two weeks at the latest. I might have a position

available by then."

"I'll be there."

When I told Dmitriy about it, he was not surprised. He said, "Take this opportunity. I can tell that you really want to work with Edie."

I was thrilled. I agreed to move to Washington, D.C., in 2006 to work for The Public Affairs Group (TPAG) founded by Edie.

While some people would wonder why a successful stockbroker would agree to move to a new city alone, I knew intuitively that any opportunity to work with Edie would be an education unto itself. That turned out to be an understatement. I tell people that my experience working with her was far harder than getting an MBA from Harvard.

"Edie, I'll be there on Monday, January 23."

"Your official start date will be February 1," she said. "One week will be unpaid."

"That is fine," I agreed. "I want some good firsthand training."

"I found you an apartment a few blocks from my house so we can commute to work together."

I took a red-eye flight to Washington, and then the subway to the Foggy Bottom-GWU (George

Washington University) Metro Station, as Edie suggested, then went to her office near Georgetown. I arrived on time. Edie opened her morning meeting by welcoming me to the company.

For the first ten days, I stayed with Edie and Joe. They made great hosts. I enjoyed dinner conversation with them. We reviewed our day and planned for the next one, preparing our checklists. They also took me around the city and helped me get familiar with the area around Woodley Park, where I live now.

Washington, D.C., is a political mecca. Everyone discusses politics, I thought.

"Are you Republican or Democrat?" the taxi driver had asked me back then.

I was silent, lost in my thoughts. I was dressed conservatively in my navy jacket with red and white stripes, navy trousers, and a white shirt with a red scarf wrapped around my neck.

I realized that I wasn't paying enough attention to my conversation with this taxi driver.

"Men on the Hill like to wear red ties," he said. "And you have a red scarf." Then he asked another question. "Are you Chinese?"

"No. I am Korean, but I'm from Russia."

"Russia?" He looked at me in his rearview mirror. "But you look Chinese."

"I hear that all the time."

I had the most interesting first week ever on a job. We were in the U.S. Senate three times. We met with Senator Hillary Clinton and all the other women senators at the Democratic luncheon at the Marriott Capitol Hotel. Everyone discussed his or her political views and concerns for our country. I was observing and learning again.

When Dmitriy came to visit me for the first time in February, I was busy working. He could not stay long for the same reason. "I wish you could stay longer," I told him the night before his flight. "Well, I can come to visit you in two months," he reassured me.

That night, we had a snowfall (the all-time largest amount of snow, ten inches, since at least 1869). I woke up and looked out the window. All the trees were covered with snow, like the miniature paintings on old *Palekh* lacquer boxes. I had never seen so much snow. The Ronald Reagan Washington National Airport was closed for a day. My wish came true and Dmitriy stayed until the next day.

I was so busy! Edie received about two hundred calls every day, and every call was important. Everyone who called was important. Edie's entrepreneurial spirit is in her blood. Her father and mother started Casual Corner stores in Atlanta, where her father had moved from New York after serving in World War II. Little Edie and her brother used to help their parents decorate Christmas trees in their stores.

One of the lessons I learned from Edie included how to handle the hundreds of phone calls every day. What was the secret? Start every conversation with "What can I do for you?" or "How can I help you?" Edie reminded our team, "Never say 'no.' Find solutions. Don't turn people away. Embrace everyone. Be gracious." Talk about cutting to the chase and saving everyone time. Her motto was "Under-promise and over-deliver."

Once again, I knew that I needed to build a relationship with the people who called us, so Edie could have more free time to focus on big projects. I inherited hundreds of press kits. Whenever I had some free time, I read and memorized clients' backgrounds. When clients called, I complimented them on their achievements, scheduled calls, and set up meetings. Edie graciously asked for their agendas, not only for meetings but for calls. She was focused and to the point. After doing this for three months, I told Edie that I used to make five hundred calls a day at PaineWebber and that I loved to sell and review business proposals.

"That is great!" Edie exclaimed. "I'll give you that for a goal."

My goal was to raise $632,000 in nine months. *A challenge inspires me. I can do it,* I thought to myself.

In a few months, I was promoted to executive director for the Business Women's Network, one of three divisions founded by Edie in 1993. By the end of the year, we had a hundred new members who were the achievers and givers. Among the organizations we worked with were the AARP Women's Leadership Circle; the Euro-American Women's Council; the Office Depot Women's Advisory Board; and The Calvert Group.

The Business Women's Network was growing, and I was growing as well. We had less than four months before our next annual event, which was called "WOW! Facts!" and was held in the Senate and the White House on July 12–13, 2006.

I arrived at the Russell Senate Office Building on Capitol Hill, the oldest Senate office building. This was a memorable day in my life. We had invited numerous political dignitaries, Cabinet members, and other people from the legislative branch; among them were

Secretary of Labor Elaine L. Chao, Senator Hillary Rodham Clinton, Senator Dianne Feinstein, Senator Barack Obama, and Senator Debbie Stabenow. Seventy top women entrepreneurs joined us to showcase their commitment to further diversity initiatives.

After the morning opening in the U.S. Senate, we had a short bus ride to the White House. We had a briefing with Anna Escobedo Cabral, U.S. Treasurer, and Karl Zinsmeister, the director of the Domestic Policy Council.

What I learned from meeting those powerful people was that they were human, just like you and me. They were highly motivated, energetic, bold, confident, resilient, totally focused, fearless, and loving people. Their success inspired me to find my own voice, to be me, and to love myself for who I am. As Don always told me, "Have faith, Lana. Faith is a path through doubt. Each of us has a purpose to fulfill." Isn't that so true?

(Don died from complications after a heart attack at the age of fifty-three on June 13, 2008.)

The Business Women's Network grew to a million-dollar division in less than a year. Edie and I traveled every week. We saw each other more than we saw our husbands. For Christmas, I received a small box from Edie. I carefully opened it and discovered a beautiful ring inside.

"It was my mom's ring," said Edie. "Please wear it in her memory. We are your extended family. We are here for each other."

CHAPTER 15
MY FAMILY ROOTS

"There are two lasting bequests we can
give to our children—one is roots, and
the other, wings."

—Hodding S. Carter

The deeper our roots, the stronger we are.

My early memories of my loving family can't be taken away from me.

I went to our family reunion in September 2007 in Almaty, where my *babushka* lives with her youngest daughter Zoya and her family. I inherited the inclination for storytelling from my grandmother.

White Pearl had been accepted to the Institute of Pedagogy in Vladivostok in September 1936. She majored in Korean literature. My grandmother was a talented woman who could have been anything she desired and hoped for. Her family lived five or six miles from a small town called Artem. Every day her little brother Nikolai walked more than ten miles to and from school.

Her other brother Moisey was married and had two children. Moisey worked at the coal mine, standing in a dark, wet, narrow space for twelve-hour shifts with one lunch break and no days off for years. Many miners lived in cabins, wooden barracks, and tents. Mining was the most dangerous work. Many were trapped and unable to get out during explosions. The water seeped into the mineshafts, the air was damp, and it smelled of rotten eggs. Moisey worked day and night to feed his family. Many of his friends died of black lung disease caused by breathing in coal dust. He was lucky to survive. His wife always saved her portion of her meal for him. According to my grandmother, Moisey's wife suffered from malnutrition all her life.

"She ate a fistful of rice and drank a bit of water," White Pearl said. "Not even tea. Tea was expensive. She was patient, kind, compassionate, and worried about her husband and children."

Grandmother explained, "Because everyone in the village did the same work, no one was more important than anyone else. Villagers knew how to hunt deer, hares, and foxes, how to bury a relative following the custom of the older people, how to build a log house, how to butcher a pig and pluck a chicken's feathers, how to flail rice for porridge, how to bake bread, how to fix a fence and build a *kolodez* [well]. Men knew how to shear goats and catch fish, and women knew how to slaughter chickens and gut the fish. Townspeople helped each other in any way they could, watching each other's children, sharing food, planting and harvesting, celebrating birthdays. They knew how to live a happy life."

"Your life was not easy, Grandmother." I gently hugged her.

"We used to grow rice, corn, beans, squash, vegetables, and the opium poppy for medical purposes." She gestured toward the bucket filled with vegetables that my aunt had bought at the local bazaar the other day. "Poppies were normally planted between rows of corn, as the corn stalks protected them from the wind. Men knew how to pierce the pods with sharp handmade knives. The sap dripped, and the men waited until it coagulated and turned brown, with the thick consistency of honey. Then they scraped and rolled it into tiny round balls, which they stored in a glass jar in case someone had cancer, poisonous snakebite, toothache, or any pain. Opium was also given to elderly people to give them more vitality and energy. One kilogram of opium was worth a year's supply of rice."

All Koreans had to buy a residence permit and pay in gold for each of their family members, including children. Not everyone had a passport. Many Korean immigrants came to the Far East of Russia illegally by crossing the Tumangan River near Vladivostok. Two-thirds of the entire population were Koreans, around one hundred thousand people. But they still didn't have Russian citizenship. They paid a lot of money for their resident permit to the Russian Government.

According to Grandmother, newcomers didn't have land and were forced to rent it from the legal citizens. "Our houses were primitive and barely furnished," *Babushka* told me. "They were built with thatched roofs by local men. The dirt floor was sprinkled with fresh water to keep dust down, and it was swept every day with a *venik* [a brush made out of bound straw]. Kennels for the dogs were located in each *dvor* [courtyard]. They smelled like urine and attracted black flies, but the dogs were needed for protection from foxes that stole chickens from the *kuryatnik* [hen house], and bears that would visit once in a while in the spring after their hibernation.

"My mother would pick good mushrooms and berries in the forest to sell at our local farmers' market," Grandmother said. "She grew vegetables and herbs to cook for us and sold the leftovers at the market. Her profit was just barely enough to feed all of us." At the time, my school lunch cost five *kopeek* (one hundred *kopeek* make one ruble). "But," she added, "we had no *kopeika*. My little brother, Nikolai, was begging me to buy him a lunch one day, so I gave him a *podsatylnik* [a hit on the top of the head]. Nikolai started crying out loud. At that same moment, the school principal heard the cry and came to the scene.

"'What's the matter?' he asked me in a sharp tone.

"'I'm sorry,' I replied offhandedly. 'He is just hungry. We have no money to buy him lunch.'

"'Come to my *cabinet* [office] now,' he ordered me.

"Nikolai and I followed him. 'I always get in trouble with you,' I whispered to Nikolai. 'Would you behave?' I didn't know the purpose of our meeting.

"'Olya,' which is what Nikolai called me, 'I have a stomach ache. I am not going to cry again if you feed me.'

"The head of the school gave me a stack of coupons. 'Here are some coupons for free lunches for your brother.'

"'*Horosho* [good]. *Spasibo.* One problem is solved.'

"'I will share my lunch with you,' Nikolai said and stopped crying.

"Nikolai was happy to go to school and was looking forward to his lunch," said White Pearl. "Meanwhile, I studied the works of Karl Marx, Friedrich Engels, and Vladimir Lenin. I absolutely loved history and Russian literature. My favorite poets were Alexander Pushkin and Mikhail Lermontov. I enjoyed discovering the world and learning new things every day, even though I never graduated."

A major event in the lives of many people would also change my grandmother's life forever. In August 1937, nearly 200,000 Koreans were deported from the Far East of Russia (the region north of Japan) because Joseph Stalin suspected that they would spy for the Japanese. Stalin was getting ready for what would become World War II. Many of the Koreans were sent to labor camps and coal mines in Karaganda, Kazakhstan, by cattle trains. Each train had a number to track the location of the deportation and the arrival day. The cattle trains had no windows. They had two-level plank beds and a stove and held five to six families. Many Communist activists were sent to the Gulag, which was the Russian acronym for the Chief Administration of Corrective Labor Camps and Colonies. Agents were actively looking for people who would complain about the deportation, so White Pearl kept silent when she heard about the deportations from her neighbors. People were evacuated on short notice. The massive 1937 deportation took just three months. The commissars waited until the harvest was gathered, then packed people into crowded cattle cars that were sent off to the unsettled land almost 3,700 miles away. Thousands, including children, perished from starvation, disease, and the effects of cold weather.

"We were deprived of basic rights and freedoms," *Babushka* said. "We had no right to choose a place to live, a job, or get an education. All of us were left destitute."

I am not a scholar. This is my grandmother's story. As I write this, I still have many questions, and I have the feeling that I will never stop looking for answers. The deportation of Soviet Koreans had remained under a ban for more than half a century until the era of *glasnost,* and scholars and researchers have only been studying this topic for the past ten to fifteen years. However, I felt that I had to tell the story of my grandmother the way she told me. She doesn't remember the day of her wedding, but she remembers the day of deportation and the train as if it were yesterday.

"I was at the institute in Vladivostok that day," Grandmother remembered. "My family was deported on a sunny day. It was August 18, 1937. When I arrived home that evening and walked into the house, rice was spilled all over the kitchen floor and a few empty buckets were lying near the stove, which was already cold. The pot of cooked rice and soup were untouched. The garden was stripped of its crops. *Where is my little Nikolai?* I thought. Our neighbor Elena, who was a sewing woman at the local factory, walked in and said to me, 'Olga, he is gone. He was on the first train that left this morning. I don't know where exactly it was going, but I heard that it went to Kazakhstan.' I spent the night in an empty house. I recalled the day my father asked me to take care of Nikolai when he left for China in the winter of 1931.

"Early the next morning," White Pearl continued, "I paid the taxes on the crops and went to the institute. My neighbors were teachers, and they waited for me. Our train left Vladivostok on September 22, 1937, at two o'clock in the afternoon.

"I heard that the construction of the Trans-Siberian Railroad had begun in 1891, and the station in our city of Vladivostok opened to the public in 1894. Turrets crowned the roof of that building, and it had majolica and tile panels and golden yellow walls. Even the Russian Tsar came to visit the Vladivostok train station. I have heard that the building was, and may still be, the most gorgeous among all the train stations built along the Trans-Siberian Railroad."

My grandmother paused in her story. Then she said, "I will never forget the sight of a woman standing on a bridge, crying. Her husband was leaving with a younger wife and children. They got on a train. The older wife wailed, 'Please, don't leave me. Take me with you.'" I wondered what had happened to her after that.

"She committed suicide," White Pearl told me a moment later. "She jumped off the bridge. In all the chaos of the deportations, no one noticed. The cattle trains were like cans of *seledka* [herring]. I don't know how I survived. During those cold nights, we slept on a stack of hay, hugging each other to protect ourselves from the cold. We could hear mice squeaking when the train stopped. *Maybe they are hungry, too,* I thought.

We didn't know how long the ride was or where we were going. There was no place for us to cook, and we felt especially bad for the small children and older people. We arrived in Kzyl-Orda, Central Asia, on October 16, 1938, at 6 a.m. When the train stopped at the station, I was glued to the door, looking for my Nikolai. It was a cold autumn. I would have given my life for him."

My grandmother took a deep breath. Her voice started to wobble.

"It was midnight. Sick people were pushed off the trains and no one buried them if they died. Those who did survive are unknown, but they are the real heroes to me. They were ordinary people, but they survived in extraordinary times. We called those trains 'ghost trains.' The ghosts still wander around because so many were left unburied. Their spirits are restless. I still dream about the ghost trains...I hear the rattle of the wheels and the patter of rain on the roof of the train.

"I saw a boy carrying a little bag. It was Nikolai! Someone had told him that the train with students and teachers from our institute had left Vladivostok a month ago. He had refused to leave the station. He was wearing a little *kepka* [cap] and a long coat with the sleeves rolled up. He had lost so much weight."

At this point, my grandmother fell silent. Her eyes told me all.

"We ran into each other's arms," she finally said. "I cried like a child. Nikolai gave me the food he had been saving for me…just pieces of bread covered with mold." She took a long breath. Her gaze was far away.

"'Look,' he said, 'I have some kernels of corn for you. I kept them dry in my pockets. I knew you would find me. We can eat them or plant them.' Wild joy from being alive and finding my youngest brother is still part of who I am today. I had promised my father to take good care of Nikolai when he left for China. I kept my promise.

"When we arrived at the steppes [the flat, and arid lands in Kazakhstan]," she continued, "there were no shelters for newcomers. We didn't have tools to build houses, so we lived in holes for the first year. Then the snow came. We burned dry grass for heat. Only a few of us survived that first cold winter. More people died there than on the ghost trains.

"A few years later, we built *kolkhoz* [collective farms] where boys between twelve and sixteen were required to work at least fifty days a year. People opened dancing clubs, formed reading groups, and even started singing classes. We faced every situation with faith, hope, and love.

"The deportation was a memorable part of our lives. Despite this difficult time, we valued education, friendship, good families, well-fed kids, happy parents, hard work, cooked meals, clean clothes, and a good night's sleep. No one could take our hope away from us!"

My grandmother, who cannot sleep through the night, longs for a restful sleep. She used to tell me that she always felt a burning sensation in her feet even at night, probably after her long days of standing. Grandmother would always stick her feet out from the heavy blanket.

White Pearl left her first husband, who was an editor of a local Korean newspaper. She was embarrassed to ask for a divorce because it was not approved of by those in her community and Korean culture.

"He was handsome," she said, "but I think inner beauty matters more. He had mistresses. He was a great dancer and spent all the weekends at the local dancing club. I had married a man whom I didn't love. I felt empty. I was scared to tell my mother that my marriage was not working. Many women were abused in their marriages, but they kept it to themselves. I didn't want to live all my life with a man I didn't love. I didn't want to have children with a man I didn't love. The best part of the deportations was that I met your grandfather, Alexander."

One of her friends introduced them. They got married the same year and had been married for forty-nine years at the time of his death in October 1986.

"Tell me about your first date," I asked her.

"We went to see a movie," she replied with a smile and blushed.

"Who took the first step?"

"Your grandfather came over one evening and made a proposal to me."

"Please tell me about my aunt Ludmila."

"I delivered my first child, your aunt Luda, at home. I'd had kidney problems after the deportation, but my health was getting better. I was ready to adopt a son, the oldest child of my husband's brother. I had a hard time conceiving my first child. We tried for four years. The rest of my children were conceived easily, and I carried three more children with ease. Luda was born on a hot summer Sunday. I made rice and soup with cabbage, baked some squash, and fried some catfish. My water broke early in the morning, and I felt like I was losing some blood. I had two buckets of hot water and three buckets of cold water in the kitchen. We had a blue washstand in the corner with a basin and an urn with water, and a separate basin was prepared for bathing the baby. I had ironed the set of sheets and towels a few days earlier. The closest hospital was a few kilometers from our house and I was home alone, but luckily I knew a midwife who lived close by and came to check on me.

"'Push!' shouted the midwife. 'Olga, push harder! I can see the baby's head. Come on!' Luda was born on the first day of the beginning of World War II. I heard the radio announcement on Sunday, June 22, 1941, from *Politburo*:

> *CITIZENS OF THE SOVIET UNION:*
> *The Soviet Government and its head, Comrade Stalin, have authorized me to make the following statement. This morning at four o'clock, without any claims having been presented to the Soviet Union, without a declaration of war, German troops attacked our country, attacked our borders at many points, and bombed our cities, Zhitomir, Kiev, Sebastopol, Kaunas, and some others from their airplanes, killing and wounding over two hundred persons. The government calls upon you, citizens of the Soviet Union, to rally still more*

closely around our glorious Bolshevist party,
around our Soviet government, around our great
leader and comrade, Stalin. Ours is a righteous
cause. The enemy shall be defeated. Victory will
be ours.

"*One thing at a time,* I thought. I had just delivered my first baby. I would deal with the war later. Luda [which is short for Ludmila] was born healthy. All I wanted was a healthy baby. I remember her first tooth, her first step, her first smile, her first curls, her first word—'Mama.' She will be always my first baby."

We had a family reunion in September 2007. I spent as much time with my aunt Ludmila as I could.

"I moved to Leningrad in 1960," Aunt Luda told me. "I worked for my dad for two years prior to applying to the Lensovet Institute of Technology in Leningrad. I graduated in 1967 as a chemist. Your father graduated from high school in 1964 and came to Leningrad to pursue his dream. My youngest sister, Zoë, was still back home. I received a scholarship. You had to be an A student to qualify for a scholarship. My only child, Irina, was born in February 1964. My husband, Marat, graduated from Leningrad Gorny Institute [Institute of Mining Industry] as an engineer. I was raising a child when I was a student. I always remember our mother, how she raised all four of us during the difficult times. We all pursued a higher education. It was not easy. Life is not easy. You just did the best you could."

Meanwhile, my grandfather Alexander was in charge of a few collective farms that grew rice. One of his collective farms was twenty kilometers away from his home. He had no car, but his horse was young and fast.

"It was the most ferocious war," White Pearl recalled. "It's hard to comprehend. The world lost roughly seventy-two million people. Russia alone lost twenty million men, women, children, senior citizens, and young people. However, Soviet Koreans were prohibited from serving in the war because Stalin didn't trust us.

"Our collective farm supplied rice and wheat to our soldiers. Even today, grain and livestock are the most important agricultural commodities. Your grandfather received an Order of the Badge of Honor in 1944. He would come home and drop on the bed exhausted with his boots on. No one dared to wake him up until the next morning. After the war was over, our second child was born. That was your father, Alexander Alexandrovich. I named him after my husband, your grandfather. Your daddy was born on June 18, 1946. Two years later Zoë, your auntie, was born on October 26, 1950. I was busy taking care of three children. I was working at a kindergarten and later as a preschool teacher. My husband was working days and nights. I was lucky that our children were obedient and healthy. I carried your father on my back tied with a piece of cloth around my waist. I didn't do that with my daughter Zoë after I heard that it would make a girl have crooked legs like a wheel."

My father loved to make *shashlik*, a popular dish throughout Russia. Any kind of meat could be marinated with vinegar or wine, then put on skewers.

"It is a good dish for a big family. Try this one," he said and let me taste his *shashlik*.

"It is too hot." I handed it back to him. "Can you barbeque ears of corn?"

"I can try. Why not?"

I ran to the garden to pick some corn and he roasted it. It was delicious.

"Anything you cook on a fire has an amazing flavor," my father taught.

"Mama," my father said to my grandmother at the family reunion, "I still remember when Dad brought *aport* [a special kind of apple that grows in Kazakhstan]. They were big, red, crispy apples. The suitcase in which he carried them had a fresh scent of apples for at least five years."

"Your father loved apples." White Pearl took a slice of freshly cut apple from her plate. "The first thing he did when we built our home after the war was to plant apple trees. He loved to pick apples right from the tree to eat. He always said, 'They smell like honey.'

"The traditional cultural morals of the Kazakh people were aligned with ours. They respected elders and hospitality. Strangers were welcomed. Your grandfather became fluent in the Kazakh language. He enjoyed public speaking and was very good at it. We thought that we would stay there forever. Unfortunately, we were exiled to Checheno-Ingushetiya from 1953 to 1958. We moved nineteen times and lived everywhere, from the Far East of Russia to Chechnya.

"Life tested me again," continued my grandmother. "Your Aunt Luda, Aunt Zoya, and your father, Sasha [short for Alexander] and I were waiting for your grandfather at the train station. My husband went to get a bowl of *borscht*. All of us were hungry and had only a few rubles to spend. My husband had no job. We had left all of our friends, our house, cattle, dogs, dishes, and clothing behind and we had no place to stay in Chechnya. And we had three children on our hands." Grandmother looked at me and said, "I am happy that your future will be brighter than ours."

Grandmother went back to her story. "Luda asked me where her father was. I told her he'd be right back. A few minutes later, the station operator announced that a train to Grozny would be delayed because of a horrible accident. A train had hit a man. I had a feeling I knew who it was."

"Dad." I turned to my father. "Do you remember that day?"

"I was only seven years old. The wheels of the train were taller than I was. The bolts were as big as my fist. I saw an empty *misku* [bowl] on the other side of the rail. The piece of bread was soaked with my father's blood. The wheel cut off his left arm. My mother's face was white as rice cakes. My father was unconscious, and we didn't know if he would survive. We took him to the local emergency room in the city of Syzran. Father was there for sixteen days. My father lived with nightmares for rest of his life. No one could sleep in a room with him. Your grandfather remembered the day he was hit by the train until he died. He refused to accept the disability pension because it would not be enough to feed his three children and wife," my father said and went outside to smoke a cigarette. I could tell it was still difficult for him to talk about this.

"My children and I were in shock," my grandmother said as she looked at the photograph of her husband, my grandfather. "But my husband didn't let any of us down. His spirit was strong as steel. 'I am not disabled,' he told the doctor at the hospital. 'This is just a little inconvenience. Can I go now?'

"It was a miracle," she said as she looked out of the window at the growing apple tree. "We made it to our final destination and your grandfather completed the task assigned to him. He built a good team. He treated everyone with respect, and they treated him with respect. After that, your grandfather was offered a position as a senior agriculturist back in Kzyl-Orda. Mr. Kunayev, a former First Secretary of the Kazakh Communist Party, offered him a GAZ-Volga car, but he politely said, 'No, thank you. How can I drive with one arm?'

"The spirit left his body that moment of the accident." Grandmother clasped her hands.

"Yeahhh…there was too much on his mind that day. He didn't even hear the approaching train, the whistles, the operator announcing a man on the rails. He was worried about our future and our children's future." Grandmother turned to my father and my aunts. "Your father was positive and enthusiastic," she told them. "A year later," she added, "I got pregnant, and your youngest brother, Arkadiy, was born.

"My husband Alexander was born on May 5, 1911, in Chuson, Korea." White Pearl gave us some more family history. "It's now South Korea. Your father and his brother, Andrei, went to Chelyabinsk, near the Ural Mountains. He was accepted to the College of Agriculture. A year before graduation, he was diagnosed with pleurisy and became seriously ill. His right lung did not function properly, and his right shoulder was slightly lower than his left shoulder."

I had heard that my grandfather's older brother was in China. He was a gambler. When he lost a game, some men came in the next morning and cleaned out the house. The family was bankrupted.

"After the train accident," my grandmother continued, "my husband worked with one arm. He never complained. He managed to ride a horse, his fastest transportation, with one arm. He continued working long hours. He cleaned his own room. It was always in *poryadke* [order]. He kept his reading glasses, envelopes, stamps, and a long wooden stick with a dry ear of corn on the end (to scratch his back) on a windowsill. He never missed a day reading *Pravda*. He was up on all the news from the Kremlin."

My father gave me some more information. "Your grandfather went to Moscow every year for the next five years to visit *Vystavka Dostizheniy Narodnogo Khozyastva* (VDNH), an exhibition of national economic achievements."

"Yeahhh," said White Pearl. "He was a lucky man." Her favorite sounds were "Yeahhh…" (when she spoke of things that related to benevolent spirits) and "Yeeee…"(when bad luck was at play). "My husband, Alexander"—Grandmother's voice was full of joy— "met a lonely old Korean couple who had lost their only son and whose entire family had been dispersed. They were so happy to have met my husband that they gave him a brand-new sewing machine, for me, and a pair of rare velvet antlers from a wild reindeer from Vladivostok. Alexander drove to their house to thank them, bringing a few pounds of rice, flour, and sugar.

"These antlers saved our lives! People have used them for medical purposes for two thousand years. The Chinese called them 'in front of the eyes'; Russians called them 'horns of gold.' The old Korean woman shared her recipes for making a *yagi* [drug]." White Pearl opened her notebook with recipes. "I chopped the antlers into small pieces and cooked them in an iron pot for a few days. Grandfather and I drank the dark brown broth and recovered quickly from the *plevrit* [pleuritis]. I'm so grateful to the old couple. *Mir ne bez dobryh ludei* [The world is not without good people]."

CHAPTER 16
COMING INTO MY OWN

"I've come to believe that each of us has a personal calling that's as unique as a fingerprint—and that the best way to succeed is to discover what you love and then find a way to offer it to others in the form of service, working hard, and also allowing the energy of the universe to lead you."

—Oprah Winfrey

My life is daily proof that our dreams can and do come true. In 2006, at our Annual Diversity Conference, I had the privilege of meeting Dr. Dorothy I. Height. Dr. Height's life exemplifies her vision for better life, justice, and human rights for all people. It was my second time to hear her speak. At both times, she talked about her two mentors, Mary McLeod Bethune and Eleanor Roosevelt. Dr. Height believes that these women inspired her to become an educator and social activist and to be actively involved in the civil rights movement.

Dr. Height said that Bethune was born on a cotton farm in South Carolina, the fifteenth of seventeen children. Her mother and father had been slaves. In 1904, she used $1.50 to start the Literary and Industrial Training School for Negro Girls in Daytona. In 1932, she worked for the election of Franklin D. Roosevelt. She and First Lady Eleanor Roosevelt became friends and mentors for the young Dorothy Height.

I have met and worked with some powerful women entrepreneurs. I recalled how impressed I was when Edie talked to me from the U.S. Senate, and now, here I was running a Business Women's Network and working with Edie on our annual conferences in the U.S. Senate and the White House.

Me—the girl from Russia—who arrived sixteen years ago with only a dollar in my pocket and not able to speak a word of English. If only my parents and grandmother could see me now.

I could not wait to tell White Pearl that while I didn't see Liza Minnelli sing on Broadway as we had originally planned the evening she gave me her heirloom necklace and earrings, I did see her at our 2006 Annual Diversity and Women's Leadership Conference, and we exchanged a hug.

At the conference in Boston in 2007, I met Mary Wilson, an original member of the Supremes (Florence Ballard, Mary Wilson, and Diana Ross), a female singing group from the 1960s. They were the second most popular group after the Beatles. She wrote a few words for my Russian-Korean *babushka*: "*Olga, Dare to Dream. Mary Wilson.*"

On December 7, 2007, my friend, Loula, invited me to be her guest at the United Nations Correspondents Association Gala at the UN in New York City. Also in attendance were Ban Ki-Moon of the Republic of Korea, the eighth Secretary-General of the United Nations, Sir Richard Branson, and many other dignitaries.

When I see White Pearl again, I'll tell her that I have realized my dream of becoming a businesswoman. That I made good on her advice to be fearless, to aim high, and to give back. That I have volunteered for many organizations including the Junior League

(San Francisco and Washington chapters), Rotary Club International, and Innocents At Risk.

White Pearl would like Jane Riley, who has been a friend for years. She was known for her *Women in Business* television show on KCBS in San Francisco. (Many call her the queen of KCBS.) Every time we talk, Jane reminds me, "It is nice to be important, but it is more important to be nice."

I'll tell White Pearl that it's a privilege to be called "American." I feel that with citizenship comes a responsibility to make this country better for everyone. It's a privilege to have freedom and be able to vote. In 2008, I became involved in fund-raising for Senator Hillary Rodham Clinton. I gained my fund-raising skills by volunteering at the Junior League of San Francisco when I joined the organization in July 2002. It was an honor to be of service.

I'll tell my grandmother that I was inducted into the 2008 Asian Academy Hall of Fame in Beijing, China. It was my first trip to China. I cruised down the Yangtze River and toured the Three Gorges Dam, which is one of the largest hydro-electric power stations in the world. I also visited the Forbidden City and made new friends.

When I see my father, I'll tell him that he was right. *Character is important.* I always remembered his advice, "When you get knocked down, you get up."

On my previous trip to Russia, my father gave me a "gypsy ring." One of his patients, who was a gypsy, said to him, "Please take this special ring for your daughter in America."

"I cannot accept this ring. I don't think my daughter wears much jewelry," my father told her. He gave this as a reason not to accept the ring. The gypsy woman left the hospital that afternoon.

"The next morning," my father told me, "I walked into my office and saw the ring on my desk. Here is this ring for you. She wished you luck." It was made from rose gold with some filigree on the sides. Did it come from the same gypsy I met when I was six years old? That I do not know.

I'll tell my father how I cold-called the Library of Congress, the largest library in the world, when I was doing research for this book, especially the parts about my family and White Pearl. Sonya Lee, reference specialist, and Hwa-Wei Lee, former chief of the Asian Division, asked me if our family would be interested in donating photos to preserve our heritage for future generations. They assured me that it would be the best place in the world for them.

When I see my mother, I'll thank her for agreeing to pay Vladimir so I could get that Aeroflot ticket, even at his inflated price. I'll tell my mother that she is the most patient and compassionate person in the world. I will tell my mother how much I love her.

My mother always worries about her six sisters and two brothers. I will tell my thirty-three nephews and nieces that they can be anything they want—if they think and dream BIG! And if they pursue their dreams.

EPILOGUE
WHAT NEXT?

"In this life we cannot do great things.
We can only do small things with
great love."
—Mother Teresa

❧

What does my future hold? Who knows? What I
do know is that our future can be triggered by standing
in line to buy a loaf of bread that doesn't exist. My
life is nothing but a string of serendipitous events and
good fortune.

What I know is that on any given day, at any
given moment, an individual or an incident can set in
motion a series of events that have the power to shape
a life that exceeds our wildest dreams and our fondest

hopes. Every personal connection has its own purpose, meaning, and reason. I believe what happened to me in America is the continuation of White Pearl's spirit. All I know for sure about my future is that I'm on my way. I'll figure it out as I go; I'll figure it out when I get there. I may even track down Vladimir and tell him what's happened to his old schoolmate. Some day, I may visit that local bakery again…

Keep in Touch!

I have enjoyed sharing my journey with you. I hope my book inspires you to savor each moment of your life, to embrace all that life has to offer, and to be forever grateful for God's precious gift called life. Please send me your inspiring stories that I may share in my presentations and speeches or perhaps in my next book. Please visit my website for more information at www.svetlanakim.com, and feel free to contact me if you have comments, questions, or suggestions. My personal e-mail address is svetlana@ svetlanakim.com.

Thank you for reading my book! *Spasibo!*

NOTES

✦

Chapter 1: An Innocent Trip to a Local Bakery (pages 19-32)

21. *Propiska* ("the record of place of residence") This system was similar to the czarist internal passport system that controlled population movements in the Russian Empire.

Everyone was required to have a valid *propiska*. After the collapse of the Soviet Union in 1991, registration system was instituted to replace the *propiska*.

21. *Kupony* ("ration coupons") They were primarily used during World War II. In 1991, shortages for agriculture and consumer goods were growing. Items that were distributed through rationing included meat, butter, sugar, household soap, and laundry detergent. Only twenty types of consumer goods out of eleven hundred were available for purchase on the common market.

21. *Banya* ("sauna") The word *banya* derives from Latin *balneum*, which means "to chase out pain." Everyone, from Tsars to peasants, were accustomed to going to *banya*, the traditional steam bath.

21. *Parilka* ("steam room") This is one of three rooms associated with the *banya*. After relaxing in the steam room, bathers hit themselves with a *venik* (a bundle of dried and leafy birch twigs) to improve blood circulation. The bundles were softened with hot water so as not to hurt the skin.

21. *Kvass* or *kvas* ("beverage made from fermented rye bread") Under Peter the Great, this was the most common beverage consumed by every class in Russian society. Later, in the 19th century, it was reported that peasants and monks drank as much *kvass* as water.

22. *Novosti* is a Russian state news agency based in Moscow that dates back to 1941. At that time, its main task was to cover international and military events and the events of the country's domestic life in periodicals and on the radio. The agency has evolved into what is known today as a Russian Information Agency Novosti and it is represented in news bureaus around the world.

23. *Belomorkanal* A Soviet brand of cigarettes that was introduced to commemorate the construction of the "White Sea-Baltic Sea Canal." The canal connects the White Sea with the Baltic Sea near St. Petersburg. Its original name was (until 1961) *Belomorsko-Baltiyskiy Kanal imeni Stalina* ("Stalin White Sea-Baltic Sea Canal"),

and it is known under the abbreviation *Belomorkanal.* The canal was completed on August 2, 1933, four months ahead of schedule and was the first major project in the Soviet Union using forced labor.

Chapter 2: My Russian-Korean Babushka (pages 33-59)

34. *Koryo-saram* (Russian: *kopë capam*) The name by which ethnic Koreans living in the post-Soviet states use to refer to themselves. Approximately 500,000 ethnic Koreans reside in the former Soviet Union, primarily in the now-independent states of Central Asia. There are also large Korean communities in southern Russia (around Volgograd), the Caucasus, and southern Ukraine. These communities can be traced back to the Koreans who were living in the Russian Far East during the late 19th century. The term "Korean" that is used throughout this book specifically refers to customs and traditions of the "Koryo-saram" people.

Regions with significant populations.

Uzbekistan 198,000

Russia 125,000

Kazakhstan 105,000

Kyrgyzstan 19,000

Ukraine 12,000

Tajikistan 6,000

Turkmenistan 3,000

39. *Koryo-mar* The dialect of the Korean language spoken by the *Koryo-saram* and by White Pearl herself.

35. *Tay taymur* ("miso soup" in Koryo-mar) This is a basic Japanese soup made from bonito fish stock called "dashi" and soybean paste known as "miso." Miso is a staple ingredient in many dishes typical of Japanese and Korean cuisine. Making miso paste is a time-consuming process, but one which White Pearl mastered.

35. *Kimchi* ("traditional Korean pickles") *Kimchi* is made from fermented vegetables. Various seasonings, and regional ingredients and recipes give *kimchi* its distinctive flavor.

45. *Kulak* The word "kulak" was originally referred to independent farmers in Russia who owned larger farms and used hired labor. Three categories of peasants included: *bednyaks,* or poor peasants, *seredniaks,* or mid-income peasants, and *kulaks,* the high-income farmers who were presumably more successful and efficient in their labor. All *kulaks* suffered from political repressions under the rule of Joseph Stalin in the

1930s.

59. *Gorchichniki* A mustard plaster applied to the back or the chest.

59. *Banki* Little glass jars that are usually applied to the back. A match is lit inside in order to burn up the oxygen and create a tight suction. This technique is known as fire cupping in traditional Chinese medicine and is believed to extract poisons in the body and balance good health.

Chapter 3: Anxiety at the Airport (pages 61-72)

62. *Pharzovshik* A word that describes an illegal trader on a black market in Russia.

68. *Pravda ("The Truth") Pravda* was the leading newspaper of the Soviet Union.

Chapter 4: The Flight to My Future (pages 73-91)

76. *Kvashenaya Kapusta* (sauerkraut) Chopped or shredded cabbage that is fermented in its own juice. My grandmother rinsed, shredded, and salted the cabbage, then placed it in a lidded wooden bucket. Heavy rocks were placed on top to squeeze out excess moisture and to facilitate natural fermentation. Wooden buckets were commonly placed outside in the yard.

76. *Zakuska* (appetizer) A sampling of *zakuska* includes several food items such as *blinis*, caviar, cheese, fish, oysters and fish- or meat-filled pastries. A *zakuska* assortment is typically served with bottles of ice-cold vodka.

78. *Borscht* ("red soup" or "beetroot soup") The most popular Russian soup, made of beets, meat, cabbage, and potatoes. White Pearl served her signature dish both hot and cold, with sour cream and a sprinkling of fresh dill.

78. *Shchi* (cabbage soup) It has been the main first course in Russian cuisine for over one thousand years. A hodge-podge soup made of meat, cabbage, carrots, potatoes, tomatoes, and onions.

79. *Piroshki* Turnovers that are stuffed with ground beef, eggs, cabbage, or mashed potatoes.

78. *Blini* The thin Russian-style pancakes (similar to French crêpes) can be smeared with butter, sour cream, or caviar, then either folded or rolled into a tempting treat.

80. *Samovar* ("self-boiler") This is a metal container traditionally used to boil water in Russia. Since the heated water is most often used for making tea, many *samovars* have an attachment on the lid to hold and heat a teapot filled with tea concentrate. It is said that

samovars were invented in Central Asia, though origins are a matter of dispute. Some argue that the *samovar* first appeared in Russia, followed by Iran sometime around the 18th century. The name "samovar" derives from the Russian language.

Chapter 5: Welcome to America. Now What? (pages 93-102)

100. *Ded Moroz* ("Grandfather Frost") The traditional character *Ded Moroz* plays a role similar to Santa Claus.

101. *Snegurochka* ("Snow Maiden") *Snegurochka* is a character in Russian fairy tales. A fairy tale about *Snegurochka,* who is *Ded Moroz's* granddaughter, was made popular by the famous Russian playwright Alexander Ostrovsky. The story influenced the libretto by Rimsky-Korsakov that was centered on the Snow Maiden.

101. *Pelmeni* ("dumplings") *Pelmeni* have a long history in Russia, first mentioned in records dated to the 16th century. Origins are unclear. One theory suggests that explorers in the Ural Mountains discovered them. Another claims that hunters concocted *pelmeni* as a simple and nourishing food to carry along on hunting expeditions. *Pelmeni* are made from minced pork and/or beef that is wrapped in thin dough, then cooked in boiling water.

Chapter 15: My Family Roots (pages 251-273)

261. *Kolkhoz* ("collective farm") *kolkhoz* was a component of the so-called socialized farm sector that began to emerge in Soviet agriculture after the October Revolution of 1917 as an antithesis to individual or family farming. The 1920s were characterized by spontaneous and apparently voluntary emergence of collective farms, which included an updated version of the traditional Russian "commune," the generic "farming association" (*zemledel'cheskaya artel'*), the Association for Joint Cultivation of Land (TOZ), and finally the *kolkhoz*. This peaceful and gradual shift to collective farming after the October Revolution turned into a violent stampede during the forced collectivization campaign that began in 1928.

272. *VDNH* (Exhibition of Achievements of the National Economy) The exhibition was established on February 17, 1935. During Soviet times, the VDNH hosted more than 300 national and international exhibitions, and academic conferences. The events attracted over 11 million visitors annually, including 600,000 guests from outside the Soviet Union.

RESOURCES

4 Soviet Republics Defy Gorbachev on Currency, January 25, 1991, *The New York Times* (http://query. nytimes.com/gst/fullpage.html?res=9D0CEFDF17 31F936A15752C0A967958260).

Chung, Y. David, and Matt Dibble. *Koryo Saram: The Unreliable People*, a film. www.koryosaram.net/ about_film.html.

Exchange Rate Cut for Ruble, November 4, 1991, *The New York Times* (http://query.nytimes.com/gst/ fullpage.html?res=9D0CE7D71039F937A35752C 1A967958260).

Grant, Bruce. *In the Soviet House of Culture: A Century of Perestroikas* (Princeton, NJ: Princeton University Press, 1995). Horn, Sam. www.samhorn.com.

Jung-En Woo, Meredith. *The Destruction of The Soviet Koreans*, Article, International Institute, University of Michigan, Fall 2006.

Kim, Dr. German. "Koryo Saram or Koreans of the Former Soviet Union in the Past and Present." www.kimsoft.com/kr-hist.htm.

King, Ross. "Blagoslovennoe: Korean Village on the Amur," *The Review of Korean Studies* 4:2 (December

2001): 133–176.

Lee, Steven Sunwoo, Ph.D. www.koryosaram. freenet.kz.

Pohl, J. Otto. *Ethnic Cleansing in the USSR, 1937–1949* (Westport, CT: Greenwood Press, 1999).